TABLE OF CONTENTS

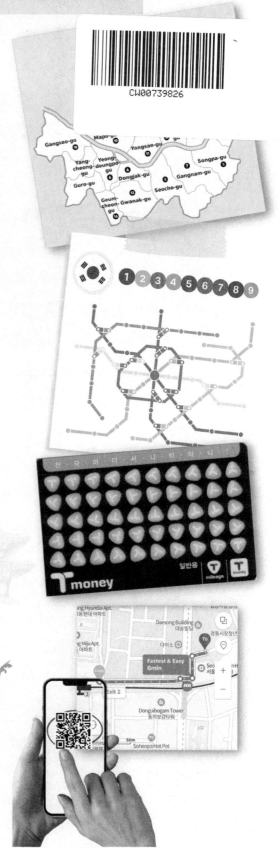

CW00739826

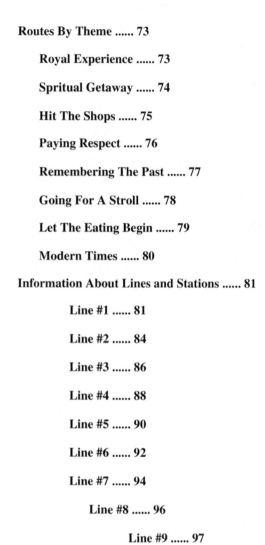

Disclaimer: Due to the constantly changing/developing nature of the city, information such as directions, time, and cost provided in this book may be inaccurate or outdated. For this reason, we strongly recommend that you not rely solely on the information contained in this book and always utilize other supplementary tools available to review and confirm the details before heading out the door.

100 Attractions Introduced In This Book

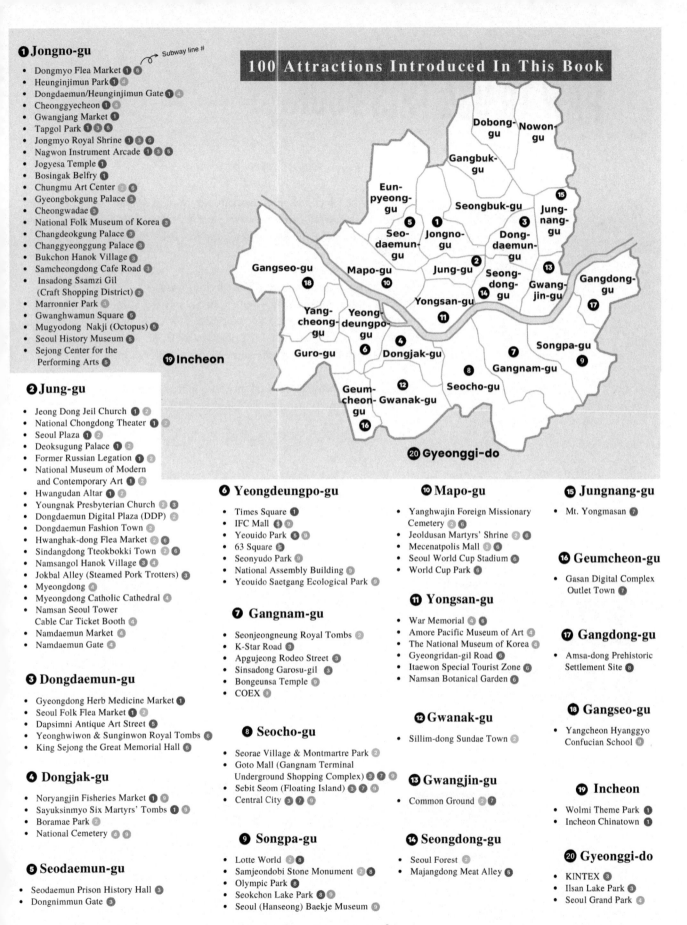

❶ Jongno-gu

Subway line #

- Dongmyo Flea Market ❶ ❻
- Heunginjimun Park ❶ ❹
- Dongdaemun/Heunginjimun Gate ❶ ❹
- Cheonggyecheon ❶ ❹
- Gwangjang Market ❶
- Tapgol Park ❶ ❸ ❺
- Jongmyo Royal Shrine ❶ ❸ ❻
- Nagwon Instrument Arcade ❶ ❸ ❺
- Jogyesa Temple ❶
- Bosingak Belfry ❶
- Chungmu Art Center ❷ ❻
- Gyeongbokgung Palace ❺
- Cheongwadae ❸
- National Folk Museum of Korea ❸
- Changdeokgung Palace ❸
- Changgyeonggung Palace ❸
- Bukchon Hanok Village ❸
- Samcheongdong Cafe Road ❸
- Insadong Ssamzi Gil
  (Craft Shopping District) ❸
- Marronnier Park ❹
- Gwanghwamun Square ❺
- Mugyodong Nakji (Octopus) ❺
- Seoul History Museum ❺
- Sejong Center for the
  Performing Arts ❺

❿ Incheon

❷ Jung-gu

- Jeong Dong Jeil Church ❶ ❷
- National Chongdong Theater ❶ ❷
- Seoul Plaza ❶ ❷
- Deoksugung Palace ❶ ❷
- Former Russian Legation ❶ ❷
- National Museum of Modern
  and Contemporary Art ❶ ❷
- Hwangudan Altar ❶ ❷
- Youngnak Presbyterian Church ❷ ❸
- Dongdaemun Digital Plaza (DDP) ❷
- Dongdaemun Fashion Town ❷
- Hwanghak-dong Flea Market ❷ ❻
- Sindangdong Tteokbokki Town ❷ ❻
- Namsangol Hanok Village ❸
- Jokbal Alley (Steamed Pork Trotters) ❸
- Myeongdong ❹
- Myeongdong Catholic Cathedral ❹
- Namsan Seoul Tower
  Cable Car Ticket Booth ❹
- Namdaemun Market ❹
- Namdaemun Gate ❹

❸ Dongdaemun-gu

- Gyeongdong Herb Medicine Market ❶
- Seoul Folk Flea Market ❶ ❷
- Dapsimni Antique Art Street ❺
- Yeonghwiwon & Sunginwon Royal Tombs ❻
- King Sejong the Great Memorial Hall ❻

❹ Dongjak-gu

- Noryangjin Fisheries Market ❶ ❾
- Sayuksinmyo Six Martyrs' Tombs ❶ ❾
- Boramae Park ❷
- National Cemetery ❹ ❾

❺ Seodaemun-gu

- Seodaemun Prison History Hall ❸
- Dongnimmun Gate ❸

❻ Yeongdeungpo-gu

- Times Square ❶
- IFC Mall ❹ ❾
- Yeouido Park ❺ ❾
- 63 Square ❺
- Seonyudo Park ❾
- National Assembly Building ❾
- Yeouido Saetgang Ecological Park ❾

❼ Gangnam-gu

- Seonjeongneung Royal Tombs ❷
- K-Star Road ❸
- Apgujeong Rodeo Street ❸
- Sinsadong Garosu-gil ❸
- Bongeunsa Temple ❾
- COEX ❾

❽ Seocho-gu

- Seorae Village & Montmartre Park ❷
- Goto Mall (Gangnam Terminal
  Underground Shopping Complex) ❸ ❼ ❾
- Sebit Seom (Floating Island) ❸ ❼ ❾
- Central City ❸ ❼ ❾

❾ Songpa-gu

- Lotte World ❷ ❽
- Samjeondobi Stone Monument ❷ ❽
- Olympic Park ❽
- Seokchon Lake Park ❽ ❾
- Seoul (Hanseong) Baekje Museum ❾

❿ Mapo-gu

- Yanghwajin Foreign Missionary
  Cemetery ❷ ❻
- Jeoldusan Martyrs' Shrine ❷ ❻
- Mecenatpolis Mall ❷ ❻
- Seoul World Cup Stadium ❻
- World Cup Park ❻

⓫ Yongsan-gu

- War Memorial ❹ ❻
- Amore Pacific Museum of Art ❹
- The National Museum of Korea ❹
- Gyeongridan-gil Road ❻
- Itaewon Special Tourist Zone ❻
- Namsan Botanical Garden ❻

⓬ Gwanak-gu

- Sillim-dong Sundae Town ❷

⓭ Gwangjin-gu

- Common Ground ❷ ❼

⓮ Seongdong-gu

- Seoul Forest ❷
- Majangdong Meat Alley ❺

⓯ Jungnang-gu

- Mt. Yongmasan ❼

⓰ Geumcheon-gu

- Gasan Digital Complex
  Outlet Town ❼

⓱ Gangdong-gu

- Amsa-dong Prehistoric
  Settlement Site ❽

⓲ Gangseo-gu

- Yangcheon Hyanggyo
  Confucian School ❾

⓳ Incheon

- Wolmi Theme Park ❶
- Incheon Chinatown ❶

⓴ Gyeonggi-do

- KINTEX ❸
- Ilsan Lake Park ❸
- Seoul Grand Park ❹

HOW TO USE THIS BOOK

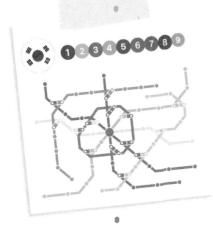

Don't go to Korea without this book!

Whether it's because of K-pop, Korean movies and dramas, or Korean food, congratulations on choosing Seoul as your next destination, where you can enjoy one of the best subway systems in the world, rated by CNN and Jalopnik.

Why travel by Korean subway? The obvious answer is that it's the most efficient and budget-friendly way to visit Seoul's top attractions. It's safe, punctual, and well-connected to cover every corner of the city. You can go anywhere you want, just by taking the subway alone, with the opportunity to interact with the local people and experience their culture!

This is precisely why we created this unique travel guide: you can visit 100 of Seoul's top attractions just by taking the subway alone!

> These markers show you where you can find public restrooms inside a station and storage lockers!

> Identify your location using station numbers!

> Station names are provided in English, Korean, and Chinese!

> Many of the stations are connected to other lines, which means free* transfers.

> You can see how far you're traveling, as well as how far you've traveled so far.

🚻	🔒	#	ENG	KOR	CHN	TRANSFER	DISTANCE (km)	ACCUM. DISTANCE (km)
●	●	201	City Hall	시청	市厅	❶		
	●	202	Euljiro 1(il)-ga	을지로입구	乙支路入口		0.7	0.7
●	●	203	Euljiro 3(sam)-ga	을지로3가	乙支路三街	❸	0.8	1.5
	●	204	Euljiro 4(sa)-ga	을지로4가	乙支路四街	❺	0.6	2.1
●	●	205	Dongdaemun History & Culture Park	동대문역사문화공원	东大门历史文化公园	❹ ❺	1	3.1
	●	206	Sindang	신당	新堂	❻	0.9	4
	●	207	Sangwangsimni	상왕십리	上往十里		0.9	4.9
●	●	208	Wangsimni	왕십리	往十里	❺	0.8	5.7

A friendly reminder about station numbers - Use the number only to identify your location because a number that is less or more than another (e.g., 302 & 803) doesn't necessarily mean that one is further in the west or in the east. Each line starts from a different point and has different routes. Do not assume that you'd have to travel in the ascending or descending order of station numbers and check the map for the location of each station before starting a trip.

*Learn more about free transfers on page 83

This indicates that lines #1 (128) and #4 (421) are connected at this station, and can be accessed from both.

This indicates only line #1 (129) passes through here.

(128)=(421) DONGDAEMUN 동대문

(129) JONGNO-5(O)-GA 종로5가

Name and address, in English and Korean.

Dongdaemun/Heunginjimun Gate
동대문/흥인지문

Jongno-gu Jong-ro 288
서울 종로구 종로 288

Dongdaemun (meaning "the east gate" and its official name is Heunginjimun Gate) is the eastern gate of the then capital city of Seoul built in 1398. The current gate was rebuilt in 1869. At that time, four gates and four rumors were built in Seoul Fortress. **Heunginjimun Gate is the largest gate along with Sungnyemun Gate in Seoul**. It has a gatehouse which is where the guard stayed, and in case of emergency, it also served as a command post in charge of the military. Outside the gatehouse, brick walls and wooden windows helped to prevent the enemy. **The gatehouse of Heunginjimun Gate reflects the characteristics of 19th-century buildings**, which have a simple overall structure but many decorations. In addition, a half-moon-shaped fortress was placed in front to prevent enemies. **The lights are turned on at night, showing off a different view than during the day.**

Cheonggyecheon
청계천

Jongno-gu Changsin-dong
서울 종로구 창신동

Before the restoration project that took place in 2005, it was just an abandoned waterway. It is now a 10.9 km (7.0 miles) long, **public recreation spot located at the heart of Seoul**, boasting its natural beauty in the thick of the busy city life. Among the **20 bridges** it has, Narae and Gwanggyo symbolize the harmony of the past and future. It passes close to Deoksugung Palace, Insa-dong Street, Changdeokgung Palace, and Changgyeonggung Palace. It is a **beautiful spot for a pleasant stroll, a fun family outing, or a romantic date night**. Lots of bushes and greenery.

Gwangjang Market
광장시장

Jongno-gu Changgyeonggung-ro 88
서울 종로구 창경궁로 88

It is **one of the most vibrant traditional markets in Seoul**, and it is easy for travelers to go because it is located in the center of the city. The traditional market with a long history formed in the early 20th century, and offers various items such as clothing and food, and the food market is especially famous. **In addition to gimbap, you can enjoy assorted pancakes, tteokbokki, and fish cakes which are made on the spot at reasonable prices.** If you are interested in clothing, it is also fun to stop by the **hanbok store** where you can see colorful traditional clothes and the vintage clothes store on the second floor.

Detailed descriptions of the place and travel tips!

4 min walk, 235m from EXIT #1

OPEN 24 HRS

12 min walk, 387m from EXIT #8

www.sisul.or.kr/open/cheonggye

5 min walk, 296m from EXIT #8

MON-FRI 9 a.m. - 11 p.m.

www.kwangjangmarket.co.kr

① Have a general understanding of the location, how to get there, and how long it would take, as well as their business hours.

② Scan (paperback book) with your smartphone or tap (eBook) the QR code, and it will open either the **NAVER MAP** or **GOOGLE MAPS**, with the location pre-set as the destination. You can simply follow the directions!

③ See the official website for more details. For the eBook, you can simply tap the link!

Seoul Subway Facts

World's longest multi-operator metro system by route length.

Rated as one of the world's best subway systems by CNN and Jalopnik

4G LTE, WiFi, DMB, and WiBro are accessible in all stations and trains

All stations have platform screen doors, adding an extra layer of security for passengers.

All lines are equipped with T-money smart payment system which incorporates RFID and NFC technology for convenient and speedy automatic payment.

Transfers between lines within the system are free.*

Full-color LCD screens that display the real-time arrival time of trains.

All stops are announced in Korean and English, and some major stops are in Japanese and Mandarin Chinese as well.

Stops are announced with cool traditional Korean music called *gugak*.

* Total trip has to be less than 10km and has to be paid using a T-Money card.
* You can transfer up to 4 times max.
* Transfers have to be made within 30 minutes after tapping the T-Money card (it is extended to 1 hour from 9 p.m. - 7 a.m.)

SEOUL SUBWAY
Information, etiquette, and tips

HOW TO SPOT SUBWAY STATIONS

Each subway station has multiple exits that are labeled with numbers.

If you're meeting someone, these exit numbers are a convenient way to decide where to meet.

- covered staircases on the sidewalks of streets
- stations are named for the neighborhood (e.g., Gangnam, Myeongdong) or nearby landmarks (e.g., Seoul Plaza).

There are spots reserved for the **elderly** and **pregnant women** and **people with disabilities**.

For all other seats, although not required by law, it's a **common courtesy to offer your seat** to those who might need it more (e.g., senior citizen, people with a heavy load)

Avoid **talking or playing music loudly** on the train.

Although not illegal, **food** should be eaten off the train.

BICYCLES

foldable   regular

Line 1-8
Foldable: Always
Regular: Weekend / Holiday
 *Allowed on **line 7** on
  weekdays 10 a.m. - 4 p.m.

Line 9
Foldable: Always
Regular: Never

RUSH HOUR
6 a.m. - 9 a.m. / 4:30 p.m. - 7 p.m.

The stations with multiple transfer platforms are the busiest, such as the EXPRESS BUS TERMINAL / GANGNAM / SEOUL STATION.

HOURS OF OPERATION
5:30 a.m. - 1 a.m. / midnight (SAT/SUN/HOLIDAY)

Some lines close earlier. Check each line's schedule before planning.

Types of Subway Cards

Single Journey Card

- One-way ride only (Not rechargeable).
- Only 1 card can be purchased at a time.
- A deposit fee of 500 KRW is refundable after use.
- Free transfer is not available at some stations.
- (Seoul Station Line 1, 4 <---> Gyeongui–Jungang line)

Can be purchased at a kiosk in any subway station.
> Ideal if you only need to take a single journey/ride.

How to Get a Single Journey Card

Find a "Ticket Vending and Card Reload Device" located in a station.

Choose your language and pick "Single Journey."

Choose your destination.

Enter the number of tickets needed and insert money.

Take the card from the vending machine.

Getting Your Deposit Back

For single journey cards, you can get the deposit refunded once you complete your one-way transit.

Simply find a "Deposit Refund Device" located inside a station and follow instructions, and get your 500 KRW.

T-Money Card

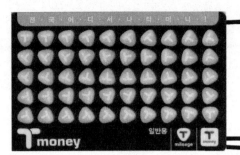

- Multiple uses (Rechargeable).
- Free transfers (4 times max, if less than 10km, within 30 minutes/up to 1 hour between 9 p.m.-7 a.m.)
- Discount also applied in combination with bus rides. (excluding buses running along the same route)
- The remaining balance is refundable.

Has to be purchased (the least expensive card is 3,000 KRW) at an outlet bearing the T-Money logo, a vending machine (line 1-4), or at the Information Center inside a station (line 5-8).
> Ideal if you plan on taking many subway rides.

KIOSKS IN A STATION DO NOT SELL THE CARDS. THEY JUST PROVIDE CHARGING SERVICES.

You can have money added to it at any of the locations listed above or at a kiosk inside a station.

Loading/Reloading Your T-Money Card

Select the
T-Money option
(the rightmost).

Place
your T-Money card
on the slot.

Choose
the amount
you wish to add.

How to get a REFUND

	Convenient stores listed above	T-money refund center located on subway lines 1-9	ATM machines at a bank (Shinhan, Hana, Woori, Jeju, Nonghyup, Shinhyup, and Post Office)
If less than 20,000 KRW remains	✓	✓	✓
If more than 20,000 but less than 50,000 KRW remains		✓	✓
If more than 50,000 KRW remains			✓

M-Pass (Foreigners Only)

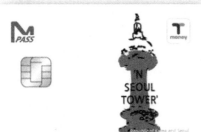

- Provides Max 20 rides a day
- Available in 1/2/3/5/7 day-pass
- Expires at midnight of the last day.
- Can also be used as a T-Money card after adding money to it.
- Deposit of 4,500 KRW (refundable) and
- 500 KRW (non-refundable) service charge.

> Ideal if your trip has a maximum of one transfer because there are no transfer discounts.
> Provides a substantial amount of savings on single-line trips.
> All purchased rides have to be used before expiration.

IT CAN BE PURCHASED ONLY AT SELECT OUTLETS

Incheon Airport Terminal 1
@ Airport Information Desk

No. 5 Gate on the 1st Fl. Arrival
No. 10 Gate on the 1st Fl. Arrival
07:00~22:00

Seoul Station
(T-money Town)

Seoul City Tower 1st Fl.
@ Exit No.10 of Seoul Station
09:00~18:00
(Closed on weekends and
public holidays)

Myeongdong

Tourist Information Center
@ Exit No.5 of Euljiro Station
09:00~20:00

Using Your Card

At every turnstile security gate, there is a card reader.

1. Place your card (Single Journey, T-Money, M-Pass).
2. You will hear the beep and the reader will display the amount deducted and the remaining balance.
3. Pass through the gate and enjoy your ride!

Subway Fares

For the most up-to-date fare info, visit t-money.co.kr

	Single Journey Card	T-Money Card	M-Pass (Foreigners Only)
		Up to 10km: 1,050 KRW	Day / Fare / Discount After 5 p.m.
Adult	KRW 100 added to the T-Money Fare	10~40km: additional 100 KRW every 5km	1-Day Pass / 15,000 / 0 KRW
		Over 40km: additional 100 KRW every 10km	2-Day / 23,000 / 20,000 KRW
Youth (13-18)	No discount (single journey fare)	Minimum charge: 720 KRW	3-Day / 30,500 / 27,500 KRW 5-Day / 47,500 / 44,500 KRW 7-Day / 64,500 / 61,500 KRW
Child (6-12)	Minimum charge: 500 KRW	Minimum charge: 450 KRW	

ESSENTIAL APPS FOR KOREA TOUR

SUBWAY KOREA

Provides the latest subway map of Seoul and all subway maps provide real-time transit, timetable, transfer information, as well as an optimal route calculator. **KOR/ENG/JPN/CHN**

KOREA SUBWAY INFO: METROID

Provides essential information such as timetable, optimal route calculator, and station information. **ENG/KOR/JPN/CHN/IND/MAL**

NAVER MAP

From turn-by-turn directions to train schedules to nearby bathroom locations, this app provides everything you need for getting around Korea. **KOR/ENG/CHN/JPN**

GOOGLE MAPS

This global navigation app provides similar features as the NAVER MAP, but it currently *does not* provide "walking" directions in Korea (things might change in the future). It does, however, provide subway directions and a list of nearby places in the languages not supported by the NAVER MAP. We suggest that you use this not as an alternative but as a supplement to the NAVER MAP.

PAPAGO

This AI-based app provides superb translation especially in Korea, which is a must when you're traveling in Korea. **KOR/ENG/JPN/CHN/ESP/FRA VTN/THA/IND/RUS/GER/ITA**

1330 Travel Hot Line
+82-2-1330 (KOR, ENG, JPN, CHN) -Friendly operators are available to answer your question!

HOW TO USE THE APPS

NAVER MAP - Changing Language

1 Open the app and find the settings icon at the top left corner.

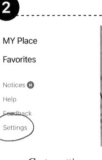

2 Go to settings at the bottom of the menu.

3 Select Language.

4 Choose from the available options.

Finding Directions Using QR Codes

1 At the bottom of each section, locate the QR code with "NAVER MAP."

2 With an eBook, tap the QR code. With a paperback book, scan the QR code with your smartphone.

3 The NAVER MAP will open up, with the location pre-set as the destination. Choose the "walk" option.

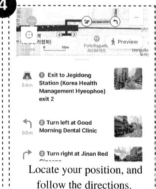

4 Locate your position, and follow the directions.

OR

At the bottom of each section, locate the QR code with "GOOGLE MAPS."

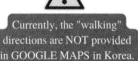

Currently, the "walking" directions are NOT provided in GOOGLE MAPS in Korea.

The GOOGLE MAPS will open up, with the location pre-set as the destination. Choose the "directions" option.

Locate your position, and follow the subway directions.

Finding Directions Manually

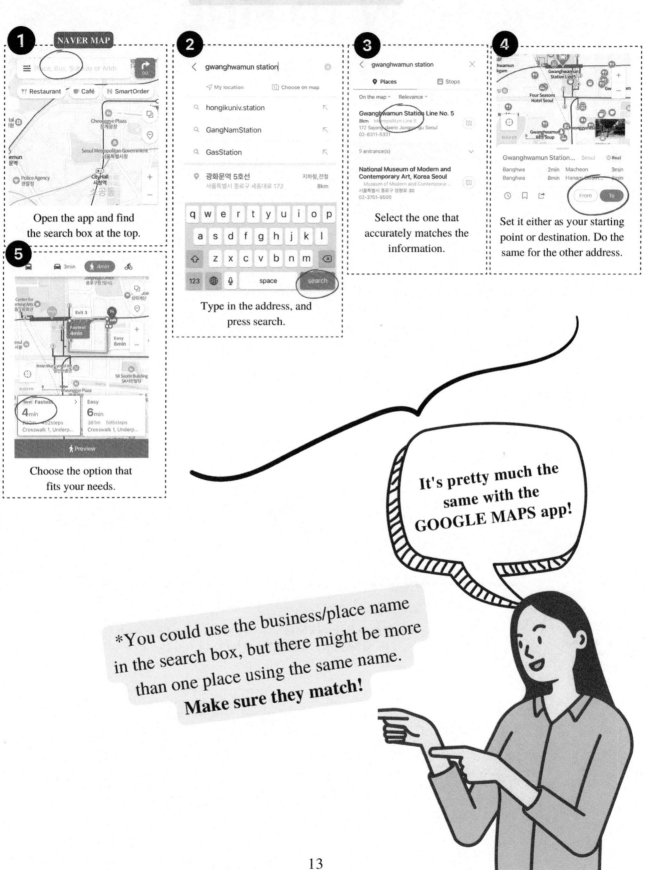

1 NAVER MAP

Open the app and find the search box at the top.

2

gwanghwamun station

Type in the address, and press search.

3 gwanghwamun station

Select the one that accurately matches the information.

4

Set it either as your starting point or destination. Do the same for the other address.

5

Choose the option that fits your needs.

It's pretty much the same with the GOOGLE MAPS app!

*You could use the business/place name in the search box, but there might be more than one place using the same name.
Make sure they match!

HOW TO FIND PUBLIC RESTROOMS

If you're already on a train...

Each subway station in Seoul has a public restroom, which is open to anyone and is completely free, so you *can* just run to a subway station near you, but here's the catch - It may have a toilet **inside** the ticket gate or **outside** the ticket gate, which means that if you're already on a train, then it's best to find one that's **inside** the ticket gate because you don't have to leave the loop for the restroom and pay again to get back in.

However, what you can do instead of leaving the loop, you can just walk up to the ticket gate (turnstile), and ask the staff member on duty to open up the side gate to get to the restroom. And when you're back, ask the person to let you back in.

Or, if there's no one on duty, there should be an intercom button. Press the button and ask the same thing, and you will have no problem getting in and out without having to leave the loop.

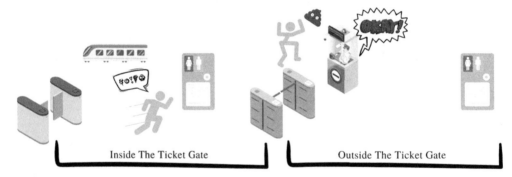

Inside The Ticket Gate   Outside The Ticket Gate

Public Restroom Inside The Ticket Gate

For your convenience, on the List of Subway Stations section on page ***, we marked every station with a public restroom **INSIDE THE TICKET GATE** so you can access them fast without having to leave the ticket gate and come back in!

🚻	🔓	#	ENG	KOR	CHN	TRANSFER	DISTANCE (km)	ACCUM. DISTANCE (km)
		131	Jonggak	종각	钟阁		0.8	48.6
●		132	City Hall	시청	市厅	2	1	49.6
		133	Seoul Station	서울역	首尔(站)	4	1.1	50.7
●		134	Namyeong	남영	南营		1.7	52.4
●		135	Yongsan	용산	龙山		1.5	53.9

If you're outside of a subway station...

1

Open Naver Map and tap the positioning icon to find your current location.

Type in "public restroom" or "화장실" in the search box.

Zoom in to locate the one nearest to you.

2

Cafes & Fast Food Restaurants
(Hit or Miss - Some are for guests only)

3

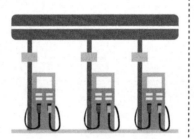

Gas Stations
(Required to have a public restroom)

4

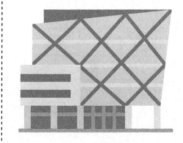

Department Stores

5

Public Offices & Universities
City hall, district office, universities, and etc.

Public Safety Boxes
At Subway Stations

What are they?

One of the plights of a traveler is having to carry around lots of luggage! For subway travelers like you, it's even more so. Luckily, Korean subway stations offer a storage facility.

Important Facts

Prohibited Items

- Cash payment is not possible - Card / T-Money only!
- There are a few stations that don't offer the service.
- Check the list.
- The maximum is five days. Any items left for more than five days will be moved to a different location. If more than five days ARE needed, call customer service in advance at 1877-1265
- Hours : 7 a.m.-1 a.m. (next day) / 7 a.m. - MIDNIGHT (Sunday/holidays)

Food   Valuables

Animals, Plants, Guns, Drugs

Check the list!

🚻	🔒	#	ENG	KOR	CHN
	●	810	Amsa	암사	岩寺
		811	Cheonho(Pungnaptoseong)	천호(풍납토성)	千户(风纳土城)
	●	812	Gangdong-gu Office	강동구청	江东区厅

Rates

Size (cm) (W x D x H)	4 Hrs	4 Hrs - 12 Hrs	12+ Hrs	1 Day	Long Term (1 Month)
S (500 x 300 x 600)	2,000 KRW	500 KRW/Hr	Every 12 Hrs 2,000 KRW	8,000 KRW	50,000 KRW
M (500 x 450 x 650)	3,000 KRW	800 KRW/Hr	Every 12 Hrs 3,000 KRW	12,400 KRW	80,000 KRW
L (500 x 900 x 600)	4,000 KRW	1,000 KRW/Hr	Every 12 Hrs 4,000 KRW	16,000 KRW	100,000 KRW

GET TO KNOW THE KOREAN CURRENCY

Paper Notes

The largest bill is 50,000 오만원 (o-man-won), which is roughly 50 USD,
followed by 10,000 만원 (man-won), roughly 10 USD,
5,000 오천원 (o-cheon-won), roughly 5 USD,
and 1,000 천원 (cheon-won), roughly USD.

Coins

The largest coin is 500 오백원 (o-baek-won), roughly 50 US cents,
followed by 100 백원 (baek-won), roughly 10 US cents,
50 오십원 (o-ship-won), roughly 5 US cents,
and 10 십원 (ship-won), roughly 1 US cent.
There are 5 and 1 won coins, but almost never used today.

Major credit cards (VISA/MC/AMEX) are accepted nearly everywhere in Korea.

Can I Use Samsung Galaxy Pay / Apple Pay?

As of 2022, Samsung Galaxy Pay is widely accepted in Korea, but Apple Pay hasn't arrived in Korea yet. However, there are rumors that Apple Pay will also be available in the near future, so keep an eye out for an update!

Using ATM Machines in Korea

You CAN use your debit card issued in your own country to withdraw money from an ATM machine in Korea. Look for the "Global ATM" sign on an ATM machine. Or, use the links below to search for one nearest you. (Even if it's in Korean, just type in an address in English and it will give you the details English address as well).

www.mastercard.co.kr/ko-kr/personal/get-support/find-nearest-atm.html   www.visa.com/atmlocator/

www.unionpayintl.com/cardholderServ/serviceCenter/atm?language=en

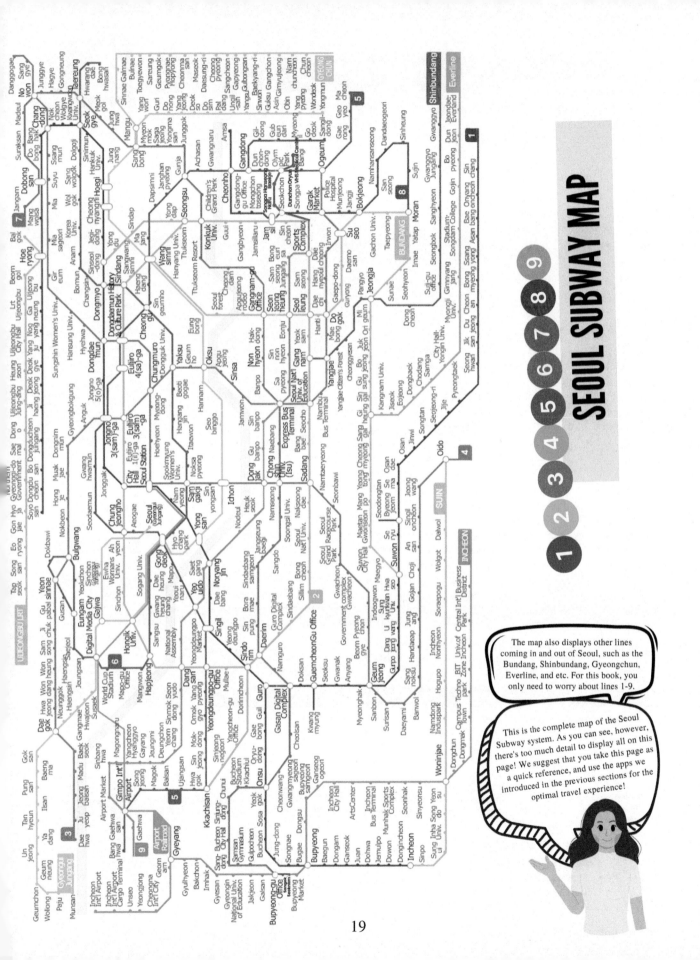

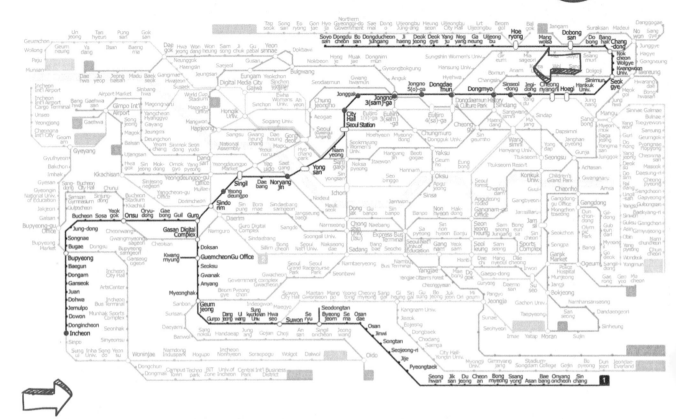

(125) JEGIDONG 제기동

- Gyeongdong Herb Medicine Market 경동시장

(126)=(211-4) SINSEOLDONG 신설동

- Seoul Folk Flea Market 서울풍물시장

(127)=(637) DONGMYO 동묘앞역

- Dongmyo Flea Market 동묘 벼룩시장

(128)=(421) DONGDAEMUN 동대문

- Heunginjimun Park 흥인지문 공원
- Dongdaemun/Heunginjimun Gate 동대문/흥인지문
- Cheonggyecheon 청계천

(129) JONGNO-5(O)-GA 종로5가

- Gwangjang Market 광장시장

(130)=(329)=(534) JONGNO 3(SAM)-GA 종로 3가

- Tapgol Park 탑골공원
- Jongmyo Royal Shrine 종묘
- Nagwon Instrument Arcade 낙원악기상가

(131) JONGGAK 종각

- Jogyesa Temple 조계사
- Bosingak Belfry 보신각

(132)=(201) CITY HALL 시청

- Jeong Dong Jeil Church 정동제일교회
- National Chongdong Theater 정동극장
- Seoul Plaza 서울광장
- Deoksugung Palace 덕수궁
- Former Russian Legation 구 러시아 공사관
- National Museum of Modern and Contemporary Art 국립현대미술관
- Hwangudan Altar 환구단

(136)=(917) NORYANGJIN 노량진

- Noryangjin Fisheries Market 노량진 수산시장
- Sayuksinmyo Six Martyrs' Tombs 사육신묘

(139) YEONGDEUNGPO 영등포

- Times Square 타임스퀘어

(161) INCHEON 인천

- Wolmi Theme Park 월미 테마파크
- Incheon Chinatown 차이나타운

A friendly reminder about station numbers - Use the number only to identify your location because a number that is less or more than another (e.g., 302 & 803) doesn't necessarily mean that one is further in the west or in the east. Each line starts from a different point and has different routes. Do not assume that you'd have to travel in the ascending or descending order of station numbers and check the map for the location of each station before starting a trip.

- **Oldest subway section in the Seoul Metro Subway system (opened on August 15, 1974)**
- **Covers a large part of the Seoul capital area. The line splits at Guro station – West to Incheon and East to Sinchang**
- **Number of stations: 98**
- **Termini : Soyosan / Incheon / Sinchang / Gwangmyeong / Seodongtan**

(125) JEGIDONG 제기동

Gyeongdong Herb Medicine Market
경동시장

Dongdaemun-gu Yangnyeong jungang-ro 10
서울 동대문구 약령중앙로 10

Shortly after the Korean War, farmers from various regions of South Korea gathered together to sell their produce, forming this market specializing in Korean medicine ingredients, dried seafood, and vegetables. A new building was completed in November 1982, introducing the largest ginseng market in Korea. It also specializes in oriental medicine. It is now well known as a tourist attraction. In recent years, there have been as many customers as Noryangjin Fisheries Market, and clothing shops (2nd floor of the new building) and flower shops (3rd floor of the new building) have also opened.

6 min walk, **192m** from **EXIT #2**

MON-FRI 9 a.m. - 6 p.m.

DOWNLOAD THE APPS! PAGE 10

(126)=(211-4) SINSEOLDONG 신설동

Seoul Folk Flea Market
서울풍물시장

Dongdaemun-gu Cheonho-daero 4-gil 21
서울 동대문구 천호대로 4길 21

Seoul Pungmul Market lost its site when the Cheonggyecheon Stream restoration project took place, so it moved to a different place in 2008. The market sells household goods, tourist souvenirs, local products, and folk food. The two-story building is full of items and food that allow you to feel the simple life of ordinary Korean people of the past. The Seoul Pungmul Market is divided into seven colors, covering food courts, local specialties, relief goods, traditional furniture, antique items, fashion accessories, clothing, calligraphy, and Korean paper. Unlike Insa-dong, there are no expensive products, and it is also a popular viewing course for foreign tourists because it is close to Cheonggyecheon Stream.

3 min walk, **199m** from **EXIT #9**

Everyday 10 a.m. - 7 p.m.
Closed on Tuesday

www.pungmul.or.kr

(127)=(637) DONGMYO 동묘앞역

Dongmyo Flea Market
동묘 벼룩시장

Jongno-gu Sungin-dong 102-8
서울 종로구 숭인동 102-8

Dongmyo Flea Market was created in the late 1980s, and its size has shrunk a lot compared to its reputation, but it is still a popular attraction where all kinds of rare items are gathered. It covers everything from clothing, shoes, and wallets to watches and electronics, even old books and movie posters. The most popular item is used clothing. Merchants usually contract clothes collected in recycling boxes in apartment complexes every year and buy them for 250 to 300 won per kilogram. Most of the clothes are priced at 1,000 won, but fur and leather are priced at 10,000 won and luxury goods at 100,000 won. As word of mouth spreads, thrifty people visit the provinces, and Internet shopping mall operators make large purchases. The best time to shop is on a holiday afternoon when more than 250 street vendors sell.

1 min walk, **86m** from **EXIT #3**

MON-FRI 2 - 8 p.m.
SAT 8 a.m. - 7 p.m.
SUN 10 a.m. - 9 p.m.

Heunginjimun Park
흥인지문 공원

Jongno-gu Jong-ro 6-ga 70
서울 종로구 종로6가 70

Heunginjimun Park was created as a park after demolishing Ewha Womans University Dongdaemun Hospital and nearby areas adjacent to Hanyangdoseong (Seoul City Fortress Wall), which was constructed in 1396 during the Joseon Dynasty era to protect the capital Hanyang (present-day Seoul) from invaders, it stands as high as 8m and stretches out 18.6km, making it the longest existing city wall in the world. Surrounding the city of Seoul, the wall is not a border but a path that connects Seoul's past and present. The 4-km hiking course is an easy walk.

4 min walk, **235m**
from **EXIT #1**

OPEN 24 HRS

Dongdaemun/Heunginjimun Gate
동대문/흥인지문

Jongno-gu Jong-ro 288
서울 종로구 종로 288

Dongdaemun (meaning "the east gate" and its official name is Heunginjimun Gate) is the eastern gate of the then capital city of Seoul, built in 1398. The current gate was rebuilt in 1869. At that time, four gates and four rumors were built in Seoul Fortress. Heunginjimun Gate is the largest gate along with Sungnyemun Gate in Seoul. It has a gatehouse which is where the guard stayed, and in case of emergency, it also served as a command post in charge of the military. Outside the gatehouse, brick walls and wooden windows helped to prevent the enemy. The gatehouse of Heunginjimun Gate reflects the characteristics of 19th-century buildings, which have a simple overall structure but many decorations. In addition, a half-moon-shaped fortress was placed in front to prevent enemies. The lights are turned on at night, showing off a different view than during the day.

3 min walk, **155m**
from **EXIT #6**

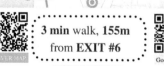

OPEN 24 HRS

Cheonggyecheon
청계천

Jongno-gu Cheonggyecheon-ro 1
서울 종로구 청계천로 1

Before the restoration project that took place in 2005, it was just an abandoned waterway. It is now a 10.9 km (7.0 miles) long public recreation spot located at the heart of Seoul, boasting its natural beauty in the thick of the busy city life. Among the 20 bridges it has, Narae and Gwanggyo symbolize the harmony of the past and future. It passes close to Deoksugung Palace, Insa-dong Street, Changdeokgung Palace, and Changgyeonggung Palace. It is a beautiful spot for a pleasant stroll, a fun family outing, or a romantic date night. Lots of bushes and greenery.

12 min walk, **387m**
from **EXIT #8**

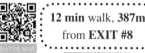

OPEN 24 HRS

www.sisul.or.kr/open_content/cheonggye

Gwangjang Market
광장시장

Jongno-gu Changgyeonggung-ro 88
서울 종로구 창경궁로 88

It is one of the most vibrant traditional markets in Seoul, and it is easy for travelers to go because it is located in the center of the city. The traditional market, with a long history, formed in the early 20th century and offers various items such as clothing and food. The food market is especially famous. In addition to gimbap, you can enjoy assorted pancakes, tteokbokki, and fish cakes which are made on the spot at reasonable prices. If you are interested in clothing, it is also fun to stop by the hanbok store, where you can see colorful traditional clothes and a vintage clothes store on the second floor.

5 min walk, 296m from **EXIT #8**

MON-FRI 9 a.m. - 11 p.m.

www.kwangjangmarket.co.kr

Tapgol Park
탑골공원

Jongno-gu Jong-ro 99
서울 종로구 종로 99

These days, it is known as a resting place for the elderly, but it is also a historical site where the independence movement took place against the Japanese colonial rule on March 1, 1919. This was originally the site of Wongaksa Temple, but it was built as a Western-style park during King Gojong of the Korean Empire in 1897. It was called Pagoda Park and changed to Tapgol Park in 1992. Passing through the main gate of Tapgol Park, you can also see the 10-story stone pagoda of Wongaksa Temple Site, National Treasure No. 2, which is considered an excellent masterpiece thanks to its colorful and unique style. At TapgolPark, you can't hear the shouts of independence, but the meaning of the day remains unchanged.

5 min walk, 338m from **EXIT #1**

MON-FRI 9 a.m. - 6 p.m.

Jongmyo Royal Shrine
종묘

Jongno-gu Hunjeong-dong 1
서울 종로구 훈정동 1

Jongmyo Shrine is one of the most refined and majestic buildings as a Confucian shrine dedicated to kings and queens of the Joseon Dynasty and their descendants. It is surrounded by small mountains and forests and consists of the Jeongjeon Hall, Yeongnyeongjeon Hall, and several annexes necessary for the preparation of rituals. The pavilion used only a minimum of color, and the decoration and technique were restrained as much as possible. This is because Jongmyo Shrine is a solemn and reverent space where the spirits of the ancestors were enshrined. Jongmyo Jerye and Jeryeak (ritual music) were listed as UNESCO's World Intangible Heritage in 2001 as "Masterpieces of Human Oral and Intangible Heritage" and have been managed as a representative list of Intangible Cultural Heritage of Humanity since 2008.

3 min walk, 299m from **Exit #11**

Times changes depending on season. Check home page before visiting.

jm.cha.go.kr

Nagwon Instrument Arcade
낙원악기상가

Jongno-gu Samil-daero 428
서울 종로구 삼일대로 428

It is the largest musical instrument shopping mall in Korea, and hundreds of musical instrument stores are concentrated on the second and third floors of the building. Visitors range from young students to professional musicians. Some specialize in selling only one instrument, such as guitar and piano, and others have various instruments, both new and used. There are expensive guitars that cost nearly 10 million won (10,000 USD), while there are also inexpensive guitars that cost tens of thousands of won. There are musical instrument-related accessories and sound devices, and there are places where you can have your musical instruments repaired at the hands of experienced experts. On the fourth floor is a "Silver Movie Theater" for the elderly and "Seoul Art Cinema," which screens independent films.

3 min walk, **104m**
from **EXIT #5**

Google Maps

EVERYDAY
10 a.m. - 7:30 p.m.
CLOSED ON SUNDAY

enakwon.com

Jogyesa Temple
조계사

Jongno-gu Ujeongguk-ro 55
서울 종로구 우정국로 55

Jogyesa Temple is the central temple of Korean Buddhism. It is said that the name Jogye was taken from Jogyesan Mountain, where Master Hyeneung stayed. It has the Mokbul Seated Buddha of Jogyesa Temple, Tangible Cultural Property No. 126, Seoul Metropolitan Government. The Lantern Festival is held in the vicinity of Jogyesa Temple and the streets of Jongno in commemoration of Buddha's birthday every year and is a good attraction for ordinary and foreign tourists. Do not miss various lantern festival events and parades.

7 min walk, **508m**
from **EXIT #2**

Google Maps

OPEN 24 HRS

www.jogyesa.kr

Bosingak Belfry
보신각

Jongno-gu Jong-ro 54
서울 종로구 종로 54

It is a traditional two-story hanok pavilion made to hang the bronze bell and has a structure of five bays in front space and four bays in side space. It was founded in 1396 and rebuilt in August 1869. It was designated as Seoul Metropolitan Government Monument No. 10 on November 10, 1997, under the name of the site of Bosingak. At midnight on January 1st, the New Year's bell ringing event is held, which is Korea's most representative New Year's celebration event. Thousands of citizens gather in front of the Bosingak Pavilion.

1 min walk, **153m**
from **EXIT #4**

Google Maps

OPEN 24 HRS

Jeong Dong Jeil Church
정동제일교회

Jung-gu Jeongdong-gil 46
서울 중구 정동길 46

Founded in 1885 by American missionary Henry Appenzeller, it is one of the first Methodist churches in Korea. Along with the Presbyterian Saemoonan Church, it is called the "Mother of Churches" in Korea. The Bethel Chapel of the Church was the first Western-style chapel in Korea and was designated as Korean Historic Site No. 256 in 1977. Korea's first pipe organ was also dedicated to the church in 1918, and Jeongdongseongga led the country's Protestant music culture.

6 min walk, 555m
from **EXIT #1**

Check Church Schedule

chungdong.org

National Chongdong Theater
정동극장

Jung-gu Jeongdong-gil 43
서울 중구 정동길 43

Chongdong (Jeongdong) Theater was created in 1995 with the historical mission of restoring Wongaksa, the first modern theater in Korea, along with three goals: the development and distribution of traditional art, the development of cultural movements in daily life, and fostering youth culture. At the time of its opening, it started as a branch of the National Theater of Korea, but it became a completely independent corporation in 1997. There are 400 seats, and a rotating stage with a diameter of 9 meters is installed in the middle of the stage. In addition, the orchestra's elevation stage was created as a variable stage that can be used as a 75-seat moving audience if necessary. It can handle not only traditional art but also performing arts of all genres, such as music, dance, and theater.

6 min walk, 439m
from **EXIT #1**

Check Event Schedule

www.jeongdong.or.kr

Seoul Plaza
서울광장

Jung-gu Taepyeong-ro 17-3
서울 중구 태평로2가 17-3

Seoul Plaza was the stage for numerous historical events such as the March 1 Independence Movement and the June Democratic Movement and was the venue for citizens' festivals during the 2002 World Cup. It is now open to all citizens, but it was only just over a decade ago that people could enter this place. Previously, Seoul Plaza was called the "Plaza in front of City Hall" and was surrounded by cars. The history of Seoul Plaza began in 1897 when King Gojong fled to the Russian legation and returned to Deoksugung Palace. To renew the foundation of the country, King Gojong built a radiation-type road centered in front of the Daehanmun Gate of Deoksugung Palace and constructed a square and an altar in front of it.

2 min walk, 91m
from **EXIT #5**

OPEN 24 HRS

plaza.seoul.go.kr

Deoksugung Palace
덕수궁

Jung-gu Sejong-daero 99
서울 중구 세종대로 99

Originally this palace was the house of Prince Wolsan but became a royal palace after the Japanese Invasion of Korea in 1592 when King Seonjo temporarily took it as the royal residence. In 1608, when King Gwanghae left for the newly constructed Changdeokgung Palace, he named this palace Gyeongungung Palace. It was used as a royal palace again in 1897 when King Gojong, who was taking refuge at the Russian legation, moved here. In 1906, the name Gyeongungung Palace became Deoksugung Palace. Here, you can find buildings incorporating both traditional and Western styles. There is also a myth that if you walk along Jeongdong-gil, also called Deoksugung Stonewall Walkway, couples will break up. In front of Daehanmun Gate, the "Royal Gatekeeper Changing Ceremony" is held every day at 11 a.m. and 2 p.m., which is a major tourist attraction. (Ticket booth located at Daehanmun Gate 대한문)

1 min walk, **80m**
from **EXIT #2**

Everyday 9 a.m. - 9 p.m.
CLOSED ON MONDAY

www.deoksugung.go.kr

National Museum of Modern and Contemporary Art 국립현대미술관

Jung-gu Sejong-daero 99
서울 중구 세종대로 99

This building was used as a museum to hold the Joseon Art Exhibition after Deoksugung Palace was opened to the public in 1933. The National Museum of Modern and Contemporary Art Deoksugung Branch was opened as a branch in Deoksugung Palace in 1998. As a symmetrical building, it has a porch with Corinthian columns. Inside the right-angled space surrounded by the east and west halls of Seokjojeon Hall, there is a garden with a bronze fountain. It is Korea's first Western-style garden and still serves as a fountain. The bench opposite the west wing across the garden is the best place to enjoy the fountain. ((Ticket booth located at Daehanmun Gate 대한문)

1 min walk, **72m**
from **EXIT #1**

CLOSED ON MONDAY

www.mmca.go.kr

Besides this Deoksugung branch, there are Seoul, Gwacheon, Chenongju branches. Visit the homepage for more info.

Former Russian Legation
구 러시아 공사관

Jung-gu Jeongdong-gil 21-18
서울 중구 정동길 21-18

This building was where King Gojong of the Korean Empire took refuge after escaping from Gyeongbokgung Palace, which was controlled by the Japanese army and the pro-Japanese cabinet, from 1896 to 1897. Most of the buildings were destroyed during the Korean War, and only the basement and the pagoda remain today. The structure is a two-story brick building with a pagoda on one side, and the style is a Renaissance building with two rainbow-shaped windows and a gable head on the four sides. Although most of the original form was damaged, it was designated as a historical site in September 1977 in consideration of its historical significance.

14 min walk, **870m**
from **EXIT #2**

OPEN 24 HRS

26

Hwangudan Altar
환구단

Jung-gu Sogong-ro 106
서울 중구 소공로 106

Sitting within the grounds of the Westin Chosun Hotel, it was a shamanistic structure constructed for the rite of heaven during the Goryeo and Joseon Dynasty. It was abolished between 1464-1897 but was rebuilt when the Joseon Dynasty became the Korean Empire.
The three stone drums symbolize the instruments used for the rites. It is a historic site that is not well-known among the locals, which makes it a good spot for photos and a place for relaxation.

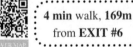

4 min walk, 169m
from **EXIT #6**

Google Maps

OPEN 24 HRS

Noryangjin Fisheries Market
노량진 수산시장

Dongjak-gu Nodeul-ro 674
서울 동작구 노들로 674

A place where you can meet the sea in the middle of downtown Seoul, which is far from the sea? It is Noryangjin Fish Market. Various marine products from all over the country are gathered here and transported to markets nationwide through auction. It is also the largest "sashimi restaurant" in Seoul. Usually, you can see the live auction taking place between 1 to 4 a.m. for wholesale merchants. During meal times, it's crowded with customers looking for fresh sashimi, but it's also a unique dating spot for young couples as well.

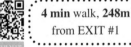

4 min walk, 248m
from EXIT #1

Google Maps

OPEN 24 HRS

www.susansijang.co.kr

Sayuksinmyo Six Martyrs' Tombs
사육신묘

Dongjak-gu Noryangjin-ro 191
서울 동작구 노량진로 191

The tomb site is for six young martyrs who were put to death as a result of a failed reinstatement plan for the King Danjong of the Josoen Dynasty. This site was made to commemorate the loyalty and righteousness of the 6. It's not an overwhelming site but always a quiet and serene place. Best to visit during the spring when forsythia and azalea are in full bloom.

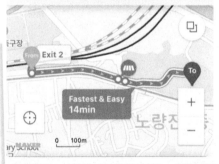

14 min walk, 697m
from **EXIT #2**

Google Maps

OPEN 24 HRS

Times Square
타임스퀘어

Yeongdeungpo-gu, Yeongjung-ro 15
서울 영등포구 영중로 15

Times Square, which opened in 2009, is one of the largest shopping complexes in Seoul, with an average of more than 200,000 visitors a day. It aims to provide a complete "malling" experience while satisfying the lifestyle needs such as fashion, culture, dining out, and entertainment. The main atrium has a large open space to the rooftop of the first floor with a large glass so that you can see the sky from all floors of the room, providing a pleasant atmosphere. Every weekend, there are various performances and activities in which visitors can participate.

5 min walk, 187m
from **EXIT #5**

EVERYDAY
10:30 a.m. - 10 p.m.

www.timessquare.co.kr

Wolmi Theme Park
월미 테마파크

Incheon Jung-gu Wolmimunhwa-ro 81
인천 중구 월미문화로 81

With excellent natural scenery, Wolmido Island has been loved by locals and tourists since its opening in 1992. Since then, it has been reborn as a massive facility called Wolmi Theme Park in 2009. Wolmi Theme Park has been featured in various TV programs such as "We Got Married," "One Night, Two Days," and "Running Man," as it is equipped with amazing rides such as 70M-high Hyper Shots Drops, Tagada Disco, and Two-Story Viking, and 115M Ferris Wheel.

The massive indoor children's play experience center Chapi Family Park, water play facilities such as mini-flume rides, water boats, water ball play, and 4D movie theaters are places where everyone from children to adults can enjoy.

39 min walk, 2.4km
from **EXIT #1**

M-F 10 a.m. - 10 p.m.
WEEKEND 10 a.m. - 10:30 p.m.

www.my-land.co.kr

Incheon Chinatown
차이나타운

Incheon Jung-gu Chinataun-ro 26 beon-gil 12-17
인천 중구 차이나타운로26번길 12-17

Incheon Chinatown was created when Incheon Port was opened in 1883 and was designated as an extraterritorial area of the Qing Dynasty in 1884. In the past, most stores sold imported goods from China, but now most of them are made up of Chinese restaurants. Chinatown is the place where the Chinese lived the most in Korea in the past.

Today, it's famous for dozens of Chinese restaurants, bakeries, and cafes, and there are many attractions such as Samgukji Mural Street, Freedom Park, and Donghwa Village.

If you visit on the weekend, you can see tourists who fill the streets and long lines of people in front of many famous Chinese restaurants.

3 min walk, 108m
from **EXIT #1**

OPEN 24 HRS

To get there faster, you can:
- Get on Bus No. 45 at the bus stop in front of Incheon Station
- Get off at Wolmi Theme Park stop. (T-Money accepted)

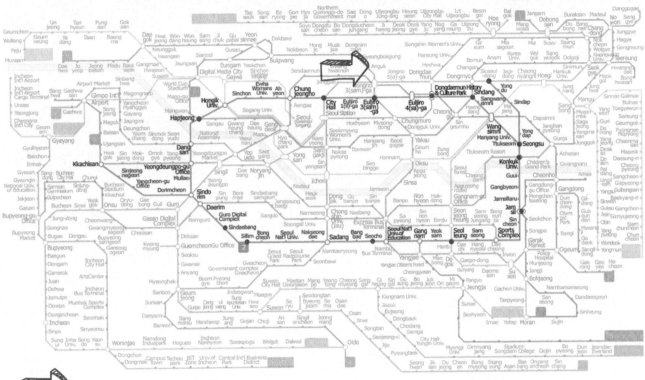

(201)=(132) CITY HALL 시청

- Jeong Dong Jeil Church 정동제일교회
- National Chongdong Theater 정동극장
- Seoul Plaza 서울광장
- Deoksugung Palace 덕수궁
- Former Russian Legation 구 러시아 공사관
- National Museum of Modern and Contemporary Art 국립현대미술관
- Hwangudan Altar 환구단

(220) SEOLLEUNG 선릉

- Seonjeongneung Royal Tombs 서울 선릉과 정릉

(238)=(622) HAPJEONG 합정

- Yanghwajin Foreign Missionary Cemetery 양화진외국인선교사묘원
- Jeoldusan Martyrs' Shrine 절두산 성지
- Mecenatpolis Mall 메세나폴리스몰

(203)=(330) EULJIRO 3(SAM)-GA 을지로 3가

- Youngnak Presbyterian Church 영락교회

(206)=(635) SINDANG 신당

- Hwanghak-dong Flea Market 황학동 벼룩시장
- Chungmu Art Center 충무 아트센터
- Sindangdong Tteokbokki Town 신당동 떡볶이타운

(224) SEOCHO 서초

- Sillim-dong Sundae Town 신림동 순대타운

(205) DONGDAEMUN HISTORY & CULTURE PARK 동대문역사문화공원

- Dongdaemun Digital Plaza (DDP) 동대문 디지털 플라자
- Dongdaemun Fashion Town 동대문 패션타운

(210) TTUKSEOM 뚝섬

- Seoul Forest 서울숲

(212)=(727) KONKUK UNIV. 건대입구

- Common Ground 커먼그라운드

(230) SILLIM 신림

- Seorae Village & Montmartre Park 서래마을 & 몽마르뜨 공원

(211-4)=(126) SINSEOLDONG 신설동

- Seoul Folk Flea Market 서울풍물시장

(216)=(814) JAMSIL 잠실

- Lotte World 롯데 월드
- Samjeondobi Stone Monument 삼전도비

(231) SINDAEBANG 신대방

- Boramae Park 보라매 공원

- **Seoul's most heavily used line - It is often packed back-to-back**
- **Circular line – running clockwise is called the "inner circle," and counter-clockwise is called the "outer circle."**
- **2nd longest loop in the world (60.2km)**
- **Connects to the city center to Gangnam, Teheran Valley and the COEX/KWTC complex Number of stations: 51**
- **Termini: City Hall / Seongsu / Sindorim City Hall / SINSEOLDONG / Kkachisan**

(201)=(132) CITY HALL 시청

Jeong Dong Jeil Church
정동제일교회

6 min walk, 555m from EXIT #1

National Chongdong Theater
정동극장

6 min walk, 439m from EXIT #1

Seoul Plaza
서울광장

2 min walk, 91m from EXIT #5

Deoksugung Palace
덕수궁

1 min walk, 80m from EXIT #2

Former Russian Legation
구 러시아 공사관

14 min walk, 870m from EXIT #2

National Museum of Modern and Contemporary Art 국립현대미술관

1 min walk, 72m from EXIT #1

Hwangudan Altar
환구단

4 min walk, 169m from EXIT #6

These places are already introduced in the previous pages.

---

(203)=(330) EULJIRO 3(SAM)-GA 을지로 3가

Youngnak Presbyterian Church
영락교회

Jung-gu, Supyo-ro 33
서울 중구 수표로 33

Founded in Seoul in 1945 by Kyung-Chik Han and inaugurated by 27 refugees from Soviet-occupied Korea above the 38th parallel, its membership increased steadily as more refugees came in pursuit of religious freedom. When rev. Han was awarded the Templeton Prize for Progress in Religion in 1992, and the number of members reached 60,000, making it the largest Presbyterian congregation in the world. The neo-gothic style building was a haven for persecuted refugees. It's not massive in size but makes a great visit along with Myeongdong Catholic Cathedral right across the street.

8 min walk, 324m from **EXIT #6**

Google Maps

EVERYDAY 6 a.m. - 11 p.m.
CLOSED ON MONDAY

www.youngnak.net

---

(205) DONGDAEMUN HISTORY & CULTURE PARK 동대문역사문화공원

Dongdaemun Digital Plaza (DDP)
동대문 디지털 플라자

Jung-gu, Eulji-ro 281
서울 중구 을지로 281

Has a UFO just landed in Seoul? This futuristic building sure will give you a one-of-a-kind experience. It is a major urban landmark designed by Zaha Hadid and Samoo. It incorporates a neo-futuristic design that distinguishes itself with elongated and curvy forms. Located in the center of Seoul's fashion hub and popular tourist destination, Dongdaemun, it features a walkable park on its roofs, exhibition spaces, futuristic shops, and restored parts of the Seoul fortress. There are three separate buildings, so make sure to visit them all.

1 min walk, 35m from **EXIT #1**

Google Maps

Everyday 10 a.m. - 8 p.m.

www.ddp.or.kr

(205) DONGDAEMUN HISTORY & CULTURE PARK 동대문역사문화공원

Dongdaemun Fashion Town
동대문 패션타운

Jung-gu, Jangchungdan-ro 263
서울 중구 장충단로 263

Dongdaemun Fashion Town, designated as a special tourist zone in 2002, is a place where traditional markets such as Gwanghui Market and Pyeonghwa Market, emerging wholesale stores such as Golden Town and Appm, and large complex shopping malls such as Duta, Migliore, and Good Morning City coexist. There are about 30 large shopping malls and 35,000 individual stores alone. Within a radius of 1km, everything from planning to production and sales of products is carried out. The scale is so huge that you can't visit it all in a day. Thanks to that, it is now very popular not only among Koreans but also among foreign tourists.

4 min walk, 208m
from **EXIT #14**

Google Maps

Each mall has their own business hours, but usually 10:30 a.m. - Midnight. Some are closed on Monday.

(206)=(635) SINDANG 신당

Hwanghakdong Flea Market
황학동 벼룩시장

Jung-gu Majang-ro 5-gil 11-7
서울 중구 마장로5길 11-7

More famously known among the locals as the "all-things market" due to its extensive range of used goods available for sale, from antiques to electronics. It's understandable why it's known as an antique collector's heaven. You can find great items at a steep discount if you are lucky. Some haggling might get you an even better deal (Try it! It's fun!).

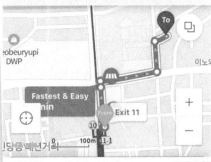

6 min walk, 392m
from **EXIT #11**

Google Maps

Usually Everyday
10 a.m. - 6/7 p.m.

Chungmu Art Center
충무 아트센터

Jongno-gu Changgyeonggung-ro 88
서울 종로구 창경궁로 88

It is a cultural complex located in Jung-gu, Seoul, named after the posthumous title Chungmu of Admiral Yi Sun-shin, who was born in Inhyeon-dong in the same district. It's known for its superb viewing environment for various performances such as classical music, plays, and musicals. In addition, there is a gallery, multi-purpose space, convention hall, orchestra practice room, local art group practice room, studio for performance practice, education space for art academy, and sports facilities such as golf practice room, swimming pool, gym, aerobics room, and shower room, as well as auxiliary facilities.

2 min walk, 105m
from **EXIT #9**

Google Maps

Everyday 9 a.m. - 10 p.m.
Closed on Monday

www.caci.or.kr

(206)=(635) SINDANG 신당

Sindangdong Tteokbokki Town
신당동 떡볶이타운

Jung-gu Sindang-dong 304-684
서울 중구 신당동 304-684

Made with soft, chewy rice cake and seasoned with spicy, sweet gochujang (hot pepper paste) sauce, it is one of the most favored street foods in Korea, often served with hard-boiled eggs, ramyun (instant) noodles, and fish cakes. Its history goes back as far as the Joseon Dynasty. History records that they were enjoyed in the royal palace, and it is still consumed today. Due to its addictive flavor, there are franchise restaurants with the name "mayak (narcotic) tteobokki."

 4 min walk, **236m** from **EXIT #8**
Google Maps

OPEN 24 HRS

(210) TTUKSEOM 뚝섬

Seoul Forest
서울숲

Seongdong-gu Ttukseom-ro 273
서울 성동구 뚝섬로 273

Seoul Forest, which opened in 2005, is becoming a relaxing resting place for citizens. Seoul Forest is divided into five theme parks, including Culture and Arts Park, Ecological Forest, Nature Experience Learning Center, Wetland Ecological Center, and Hangang Waterfront Park. The Culture and Arts Park has statues and forest playgrounds. The ecological forest combines wild animals and plants, while the Nature Experience Learning Center is composed of a Guardian Forest and an Insect Botanical Garden. Wetland Ecology Center provides forests and natural playgrounds as well as outdoor classes. Hangang Waterfront Park has a bicycle path and a dock for the Hangang River cruise ship, making it a great dating spot.

 9 min walk, **529m** from **EXIT #8**
Google Maps

OPEN 24 HRS

parks.seoul.go.kr/template/sub/seoulforest.do

(211-4)=(126) SINSEOLDONG 신설동

Seoul Folk Flea Market
서울풍물시장

3 min walk, 199m from EXIT #9

This place is already introduced in the previous pages.

Common Ground
커먼그라운드

Gwangjin-gu, Achasan-ro 200
서울 광진구 아차산로 200

As the largest container pop-up shopping mall in the world, Kolon FnC created it in 2015 using more than 200 large containers. The iconic blue container boxes are connected using bolts. Inside the building, there are sports brand shopping malls, handmade burgers, pasta, and brunch cafes. It is also considered one of the top three container architectural tourist destinations in Seoul. In line with the catchphrase of "Youth Culture Factory," where brands with young cultural sensibilities from around the world and talented designers from Korea coexist, visitors here are mainly young people in their 20s and 30s, and many foreign tourists also visit.

Lotte World
롯데 월드

Songpa-gu Ollimpik-ro 240
서울 송파구 올림픽로 240

Visited by over 7 million people each year, it is a mega recreation complex with the largest indoor theme park in the world. It houses various facilities, including shopping malls, a luxury hotel, a Korean folk museum, sports facilities, and movie theaters. It is also home to the largest ice rink in Korea. There are a variety of performances going on inside the park, which can be enjoyed at no extra cost. "Magic Island" is an artificial island sitting inside a lake linked by a monorail. It's a great amusement park and a shopping mall for people of all ages. It will keep you entertained for the whole day. Download the "Magic Pass" app to bypass long lines.

Samjeondobi Stone Monument
삼전도비

Songpa-gu Songpanaru-gil 256
서울 송파구 송파나루길 256

It is a monument erected to mark the Joseon Dynasty's submission to the Qing Dynasty in 1636 as a result of the second Manchu invasion, where King Injo had to ceremonially bow to Hong Taiji of the Qing Dynasty nine times as a servant. The Treaty of Samjeondo required that his first and second sons be taken as captives and have the Joseon Dynasty become a tributary state. It is an important piece of Korea's (disgraceful) history. It is worth making a quick visit if you are in town (Lotte World & Seokchon Lake).

3 min walk, **196m** from EXIT #6

Everyday 11 a.m. - 10 p.m.

www.common-ground.co.kr

2 min walk, **143m** from EXIT #4

Everyday 10 a.m. - 10 p.m.

www.lotteworld.com

6 min walk, **270m** from EXIT #3

OPEN 24 HRS

(220) SEOLLEUNG 선릉

Seonjeongneung Royal Tombs
서울 선릉과 정릉

Gangnam-gu Samseong-2-dong 100-gil 1
서울 강남구 삼성2동 선릉로100길 1

Seonneung and Jeongneung Royal Tombs are royal tombs in which King Seongjong, the ninth king of the Joseon Dynasty, Queen Jeonghyeon, and King Jungjong of the Joseon Dynasty are asleep. This place is historically meaningful, but the green nature is well preserved to be called "the forest in the city." When you enter Seonneung Royal Tombs and Jeongneung Royal Tombs, you will be surprised by their considerably large space. In particular, the forest path from Jeongneung, the tomb of King Jungjong, to Seonneung, where King Seongjong and Queen Jeonghyeon are asleep, is spacious. You will meet citizens walking along the trail connecting the tombs and those resting under the shade of the beautiful tree. It is a relaxing forest where you can take a break in the middle of a complex city. It was listed as a UNESCO World Heritage Site in 2009.

9 min walk, **432m** from EXIT #10

Everyday 6 a.m. - 8 p.m.
Closed on Monday

royaltombs.cha.go.kr

(224) SEOCHO 서초

Seorae Village & Montmartre Park
서래마을 & 몽마르뜨 공원

Seocho-gu, Seocho-dong, San177-3
서울 서초구 서초동 산177-3

The park was originally an acacia-wooded hill, but in 2000, the Seoul Metropolitan Waterworks Headquarters launched a drainage project to supply tap water to the Banpo area, creating a "Montmartre Park" to provide rest areas to residents through consultations with the Seoul Metropolitan Government. In particular, the park was named "Montmartre Park" because many French people lived in the nearby Seorae Village, and the access road to the village was called Montmartre Road. In Seorae Village, there is a French International School as well as many French bakeries.

9 min walk, **577m** from **EXIT #6**

OPEN 24 HRS

(230) SILLIM 신림

Sillim-dong Sundae Town
신림동 순대타운

Gwanak-gu, Sillim-ro 59-gil 14
서울 관악구 신림로 59길 14

The first place that comes to mind when you think of Sillim-dong is Sundae Town. Sundae street vendors were naturally formed and operated in the 1960s, but when the Folk Sundae Town building was built in 1992, the Sundae houses scattered in the traditional market moved into one place, forming the current Sundae Town. Unlike ordinary sundaes, baeksundae (plain) and spicy sundae stir-fried with red pepper paste, various vegetables, and seasonings mixed with beef intestines are famous in Sillim-dong, and young people often visit to eat delicious sundaes at affordable prices. Some restaurants also offer unique menus with stir-fried squid and stir-fried tripe.

3 min walk, **175m** from **EXIT #4**

Each restaurant has their own business hours, but usually 10 a.m. - Past Midnight.

(231) SINDAEBANG 신대방

Boramae Park
보라매 공원

Dongjak-gu Sindaebang-dong 395
서울 동작구 신대방동 395

Boramae Park was opened on May 5, 1986, after repairing the place where the Air Force Academy left on December 20, 1985, and became the current name of the park after taking over the symbol of the AirForce Academy, Boramae (a young hawk). Boramae Park, which represents the southwestern part of Seoul, is loved as a resting, exercise, and cultural space for many citizens as it is in contact with Dongjak-gu as well as Gwanak-gu and Yeongdeungpo-gu.

Amazing water fountain show during:
5.1 ~ 9.30
12:00 ~ 12:50 / 17:00 ~ 17:20
19:00 ~ 19:20 (lighted)
20:00 ~ 20:20 (lighted)
*Time subject to change

16 min walk, **904m**
from **EXIT #4**

OPEN 24 HRS

Google Maps

parks.seoul.go.krtemplate/sub/boramae.do

(238)=(622) HAPJEONG 합정

Yanghwajin Foreign Missionary Cemetery
양화진외국인선교사묘원

Mapo-gu Yanghwajin-gil 46
마포구 양화진길 46

From the end of the Joseon Dynasty to the Japanese colonial era, about 1,500 foreign missionaries came to Korea. They mainly engaged in medical, education, and charity work despite the Christian prohibition decree of the Joseon Dynasty. They hoped to be buried in Korea even after their deaths, so this Cemetery was created. Located alongside the Catholic holy site of Jeoldusan Mountain, Yanghwajin represents the history of the upheaval at the time, including the execution of Catholics and the decapitation of Kim Ok-kyun, a member of the Enlightenment. A total of 417 missionaries from 15 countries, including 145 first missionaries and their families are laid to rest, as well as 555 tombs of the people who worked to modernize Korea.

5 min walk, **320m**
from **EXIT #7**

Google Maps

Everyday 10 a.m.- 5 p.m. Closed on Sunday

yanghwajin.net

Jeoldusan Martyrs' Shrine
절두산 성지

Mapo-gu, Tojeong-ro 6
서울 마포구 토정로 6

Literally meaning "decapitation mountain," it is the site of the Byeongin Prosecution of 1866. History records that up to 2,000 Korean Catholics lost their lives, of which 27 have been made saints. The museum next to the chapel still has some of the torture equipment of the time. Pope John Paul II visited in 1984, and Mother Teresa in 1985. It is a truly inspiring place whether you are a Catholic or not. Sunday is the best time to visit, as there are many prayer gatherings taking place on the grounds.

7 min walk, **482m**
from **EXIT #7**

Google Maps

Everyday 9:30 a.m. - 5 p.m. Closed on Monday

www.jeoldusan.or.kr

Mecenatpolis Mall
메세나폴리스몰

Mapo-gu, Yanghwa-ro 45
서울 마포구 양화로 45

It is a high-rise residential and commercial complex shopping mall with 34 floors above ground and seven floors below ground. There are cultural spaces such as Lotte Cinema and Homeplus, various restaurants, cafes, shopping malls, and art centers in the apartment complex, so you can conveniently shop and eat. The subway is also connected directly, making it easy to move around.

1 min walk, 35m
NEXT TO EXIT #10

Google Maps

NEXT TO THE EXIT #10, there's are stairs leading directly to the mall!

Each store has their own store hours.

Dongdaemun Digital Plaza (DDP)
동대문 디지털 플라자

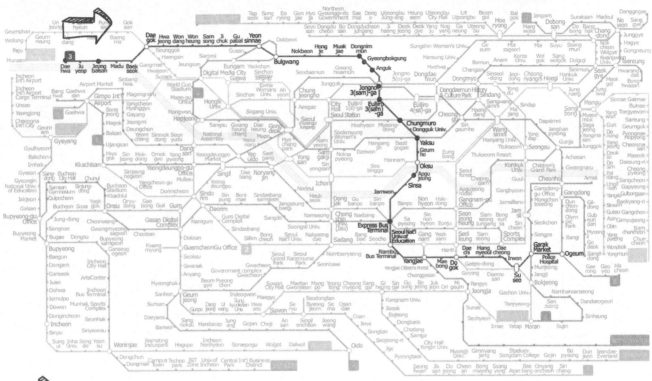

(309) DAEHWA (KINTEX) 대화

- Korea International Exhibition Center (KINTEX) 일산 킨텍스

(311) JEONGBALSAN 정발산

- Ilsan Lake Park 일산 호수공원

(326) DONGNIMMUN 독립문

- Seodaemun Prison History Hall 서대문 형무소
- Dongnimmun Gate 독립문

(327) GYEONGBOKGUNG 경복궁

- Gyeongbokgung Palace 경복궁
- Cheongwadae 청와대

(328) ANGUK 안국

- National Folk Museum of Korea 국립민속박물관
- Changdeokgung Palace 창덕궁
- Changgyeonggung Palace 창경궁
- Bukchon Hanok Village 북촌 한옥마을
- Samcheongdong Cafe Road 삼청동 카페 거리
- Insadong Ssamzi Gil (Craft Shopping District) 인사동 쌈지길

(329)=(534)=(130) JONGNO 3(SAM)-GA 종로 3가

- Tapgol Park 탑골공원
- Jongmyo Royal Shrine 종묘
- Nagwon Instrument Arcade 낙원악기상가

(330)=(203) EULJIRO 3(SAM)-GA 을지로 3가

- Youngnak Presbyterian Church 영락교회

(331)=(423) CHUNGMURO 충무로

- Namsangol Hanok Village 남산골 한옥 마을

(332) DONGGUK UNIVERSITY 동대입구

- Jokbal Alley (Steamed Pork Trotters) 장충동 족발 골목

(336) APGUJEONG 압구정

- K-Star Road 케이스타 로드
- Apgujeong Rodeo Street 압구정 로데오 거리
- Sinsadong Garosu-gil 신사동 가로수길

(339)=(734)=(923) EXPRESS BUS TERMINAL 고속터미널

- Goto Mall (Gangnam Terminal Underground Shopping Complex) 고투몰
- Sebit Seom (Floating Island) 세빛섬
- Central City 센트럴 시티

- In 2010, it recorded the 2nd highest WIFI data consumption in the Seoul Metropolitan Area.
- Number of stations: 44
- Termini : Daehwa / Ogeum

(309) DAEHWA (KINTEX) 대화

Korea International Exhibition Center (KINTEX) 일산 킨텍스

Goyang-shi, Ilsanseo-gu, Kintex-ro 217-60
경기 고양시 일산서구 킨텍스로 217-60

KINTEX is the largest exhibition and convention center in Korea and the fourth largest in Asia in terms of exhibition area. The first exhibition hall consists of one basement floor to two ground floors, and the second exhibition hall consists of one basement floor to 15 ground floors. It consists of various food and beverage stores and auxiliary facilities. It is recommended to check and visit the current events on the website.

12 min walk, 702m from **EXIT #2**

Check Event Schedule

www.kintex.com

(311) JEONGBALSAN 정발산

Ilsan Lake Park 일산 호수공원

Goyang-shi, Ilsandong-gu, Hosu-ro 731
경기 고양시 일산동구 호수로 731

Ilsan Lake Park is a neighborhood park created in connection with the Ilsan New Town housing site development project. It is the largest artificial lake in Korea that provides ecosystems that are not accessible to urbanites. In particular, the 9.1km trail, including the 4.7km bike path and the Metasequoia Road centered on the lake, provides a recreational value. In the park, various ecological cultural facilities such as an ecological nature learning center, sculptural art, and a cactus exhibition hall can also be accessed. With Goyang International Flower Fair, Autumn Flower Festival, and Lake Flowerlight Festival are held every year. It's a popular spot for tourists as well.

9 min walk, 602m from **EXIT #2**

OPEN 24 HRS

www.goyang.go.krpark/index.do

(326) DONGNIMMUN 독립문

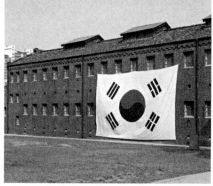

Seodaemun Prison History Hall 서대문 형무소

Seodaemun-gu, Tongil-ro 251
서울 서대문구 통일로 251

Seodaemun Prison was built at the end of the Korean Empire under the pressure of the Japanese Empire, and for more than 80 years, it was a site where the hardships and national resentment of Korea's modern and contemporary history are deeply etched on. In particular, it is a symbol of the Japanese impression of the anti-Japanese independence movement. The original shape of Seodaemun Prison that imprisoned patriots against Japanese aggression is preserved, so it is an excellent place where you can honor the sacrifice of the Korean patriots and follow in their footsteps.

6 min walk, 250m from **EXIT #5**

Everyday
Mar - Oct 9:30 a.m. - 6 p.m.
Nov - Feb 9:30 a.m. - 5 p.m.
Closed on Monday
(if a National Holiday falls on a Monday, it's closed the next day.)

www.sscmc.or.kr

(326) DONGNIMMUN 독립문

Dongnimmun Gate
독립문

Seodaemun-gu Hyeonjeo-dong 941
서울 서대문구 현저동 941

Contrary to common belief, it was not constructed to commemorate Korea's independence from the Japanese occupation. Rather, it was erected to inspire a spirit of independence from its status as a Qing Dynasty's tributary state. It was designed by Seo Jae-pil and modeled on the Arc de Triomphe in Paris. It was constructed by Afanasy Ivanovich Seredin-Sabatin, who also constructed the former Russian legation. There's a beautifully kept park around the gate that boasts Korea's pride as an independent sovereign state.

6 min walk, 270m
from **EXIT #3**

OPEN 24 HRS

(327) GYEONGBOKGUNG 경복궁

Gyeongbokgung Palace
경복궁

Jongno-gu Sajik-ro 161
서울 종로구 사직로 161

Hold your breath as the acme of the Joseon Dynasty's art and construction unfolds before your eyes. Meaning "felicitous blessing," the palace was constructed in 1395, and it is the largest Joseon Dynasty palace remaining today while being considered the most beautiful palace. Commonly referred to as the Northern palace due to its location in the northernmost part of Seoul. It was once destroyed by fire during the Imjin War against Japan, but they were all restored later.

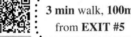

3 min walk, 100m
from **EXIT #5**

Everyday
9 a.m. - 6 p.m.
(last admission 5 p.m.)
During Sep - Nov
Night Admission 7 p.m. - 9:30 p.m
(Check website for specific date).
(if a National Holiday falls on a Monday,
it's closed the next day.)

Cheongwadae
청와대

Jongno-gu Cheongwadae-ro 1
서울 종로구 청와대로 1

Also known as the "Blue House" due to its signature blue tiles, it has been the executive office and official residence of the South Korean president until 2022, but it is now completely open to the public. It is a complex of buildings built upon the site of the royal garden of the Joseon Dynasty and covers approximately 62 acres. With the breathtaking backdrop of Bugaksan Mt., visiting the place is one unique experience you can have in Korea. Make sure to visit the homepage to register and learn about the program.

24 min walk, 1.4km
from **EXIT #3**

VIsit homepage for the latest business hours
reserve.opencheongwadae.kr

The reservation page is presented only in Korean. You might have to use your browser's translation feature.

www.royalpalace.go.kr

National Folk Museum of Korea
국립민속박물관

Jongno-gu, Samcheong-ro 37
서울 종로구 삼청로 37

Conveniently located within Gyeongbokgung Palace, it was established by the US government and was opened in 1946. Upon the merger with the National Museum of Korea, its 4,555 artifacts were moved to the Mt. Namsan site. In 1993 it opened in its present site. With more than 98,000 artifacts, it illustrates the history of the traditional life of ordinary Korean people. If you are visiting Gyeongbokgung, you must take the time to visit this unique museum. It creates a stark contrast between the life of the royal blood and that of the common people.

16 min walk, 883m
from EXIT #1

Google Maps

Everyday 9 a.m. - 6 p.m.
(last admission 5 p.m.)

www.nfm.go.krhome/index.do

Changdeokgung Palace
창덕궁

Jongno-gu Yulgok-ro 99
서울 종로구 율곡로 99

UNESCO WORLD HERITAGE - Meaning "prospering virtue," it retains many elements from the Three Kingdoms of Korea, distinguishing itself in style from the more contemporary neighbor Gyeongbokgung Palace. It was the most favored construction by many princes of the Joseon Dynasty, but only about 30% of the original buildings are remaining today, as the rest was severely damaged during the Japanese occupation. Guided tour is available. Check the homepage before visiting. Make sure to visit the Rear Garden 후원 (Huwon), which connects to Changgyeonggung Palace
(the entrance fee is 1,000 won).

9 min **walk**, 379m
from **EXIT #3**

Google Maps

Feb - May / Sep - Oct 9 a.m. - 6 p.m.
Jun - Aug 9 a.m. - 6:30 p.m.
Nov - Jan 9 a.m. - 5:30 p.m.
(Last admission 1 hour before closing)
Closed on Monday (if a national holiday falls on a Monday, it's closed the following day.)

www.cdg.go.kr

Changgyeonggung Palace
창경궁

Jongno-gu Changgyeonggung-ro 185
서울 종로구 창경궁로 185

Meaning "flourishing gladness," it was built in 1483 as one of the "eastern palaces" along with ChangdeokPalace because they were situated east of Gyeongbok Palace. It was built by King Sejong for his father, Taejong. During the Japanese occupation, they built a zoo, botanical garden, and museum right in the palace compound. It was considered an attempt to symbolically undermine the royal status of the Dynasty. They were removed in 1984. It's smaller than other palaces in Seoul, but beautiful gardens more than makeup for it. There's a very relaxing walk through the park. *You may start from Changdeokgung Palace and come through the Rear Garden 후원 (Huwon).

22 min walk, 1.3km
from **EXIT #3**

Google Maps

Everday 9 a.m. - 9 p.m.
Closed on Monday

cgg.cha.go.kr

Bukchon Hanok Village
북촌 한옥마을

Jongno-gu, Gahoe-dong 31-48
서울 종로구 가회동 31-48

Also called Yangbanchon ("Noblemen Village") because most of these high-end houses were inhabited by royalty, aristocrats, and bureaucrats during the Joseon Dynasty. In 2001, the Seoul Metropolitan Government conducted the Bukchon Conservation Project to improve the hanok and surrounding scenery and received the UNESCO Asia-Pacific Heritage Award for Excellence in 2009. It is the place where you can feel the essence of traditional Korean culture in Seoul, and even now, residents live and preserve the village. Here, you can see Bukaksan Mountain in the north and NamsanMountain in the south, which boast an excellent view. Walk between the maze-like alleys and feel the beauty of traditional hanok.

17 min walk, **865m** from **EXIT #2**

Each store has different business hours, but most open in the morning.

bukchon.seoul.go.kr

Samcheongdong Cafe Road
삼청동 카페 거리

Jongno-gu, Samcheong-ro 102
서울 종로구 삼청로 102

If you travel to Gyeongbokgung Palace in Seoul, it will be a memorable experience if you take a walk and look around Samcheongdong-gil Street on the backside. Samcheongdong-gil Street is quite elegant and busy, with stores and cafes heavily crowded. Cafe streets and shops are concentrated, and it is one of the most beloved dating places in Korea. You can see lots of hanok buildings, as well as people getting on and off the village buses at the station. It is also one of the most popular tourist attractions among foreigners.

19 min walk, **1.1km** from **EXIT #2**

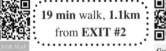

Each store has different business hours, but most open in the morning.

Insadong Ssamzi Gil (Craft Shopping District)
인사동 쌈지길

Jongno-gu Insadong-gil 44
서울 종로구 인사동길 44

Past meets present here. It is one of the tourists' favorite places for shopping for antiques/traditional goods. There are countless stores, galleries, traditional restaurants, and tea houses down along the main street. Many of the galleries specialize in traditional Korean paintings and sculptures. Just "window shopping" through the alleys is an entertaining experience. One of the best places to buy souvenirs. Many great art galleries to appreciate. Nothing much going on after sunset, though.

9 min walk, **304m** from **EXIT #6**

Everyday 10:30 a.m. - 8:30 p.m.
Closed on Seollal and Chuseok

(329)=(534)=(130)
JONGNO 3(SAM)-GA 종로 3가

Tapgol Park
탑골공원

5 min walk, 338m from EXIT #1

Jongmyo Royal Shrine
종묘

3 min walk, 299m from Exit #11

Nagwon Instrument Arcade
낙원악기상가

2 min walk, 146m from EXIT #5

These places are already introduced in the previous pages.

(330)=(203)
EULJIRO 3(SAM)-GA 을지로 3가

Youngnak Presbyterian Church
영락교회

8 min walk, 324m from EXIT #6

This place is already introduced in the previous pages.

(331)=(423) CHUNGMURO 충무로

Namsangol Hanok Village
남산골 한옥 마을

Jung-gu, Toegye-ro 34-gil 28
서울 중구 퇴계로34길 28

It was the site of a well known summer resort of the Joseon-era, which was considered one of the 5 most beautiful parts of Seoul. It consists of traditional Korean garden, along with a flowing stream and pavilion, which replicates the feel of the past. It has 5 restored traditional Korean houses, or hanok, a pavilion, and a pond. There are many activities like neolttwigi (seesaw jumping), tuho (arrow throwing) and yutnori (traditional board game). You can participate in them for free. On weekends, a reenactment of the traditional wedding ceremony takes place at Bak Yeong Hyo's Residence. Overall, it's a collection of traditional architecture that gives an insight into Korean culture.

6 min walk, 306m from EXIT #4

Everyday 9 a.m. - 9 p.m.
Closed on Monday

www.hanokmaeul.or.kr

Jokbal Alley (Steamed Pork Trotters)
장충동 족발 골목

Jung-gu, Jangchungdan-ro 174
서울 중구 장충단로 174

Similar to Zampone (Italian), Crubeens (Irish), Pied de cochon (French) jokbal is the Korean interpretation of pork trotters, cooked with soy sauce and spices. It is Korean people's favorite food to pair with soju. It is also popular among girls because it is rich in collagen which is believed to improve skin's texture. Among guys, it is popular as it is known to be effective in preventing a hangover. The whole alley is filled with restaurants serving jokbal dishes.

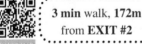

3 min walk, **172m**
from **EXIT #2**

Each store has different business hours, but most open in the morning.

K-Star Road
케이스타 로드

Gangnam-gu, Apgujeong-ro 394
서울 강남구 압구정동 394

It is no exaggeration to say that Gangnam, which attracted global attention with Psy's "Gangnam Style," is the origin of Hallyu culture. Gangnam has been a trend-leading region in Korea, and it is where more than half of the Korean entertainment agencies are located, and many Hallyu stars have been born. K-Star Road was newly built in Cheongdam-dong to commemorate this.

Along the street, you can meet a series of Gangnam Dols, which is a portmanteau word for 'Gangnam' and "idol" and "doll" because there are 17 human-sized bear-shaped statues with the stars' symbolic images, ranging from BTS, Super Junior, EXO, and Girls' Generation. As you go on, you will also pass the area where K-pop entertainment agencies are concentrated, such as JYP Entertainment and Cube Entertainment.

26 min walk, **1.3km**
from **EXIT #1**

OPEN 24 HRS

Apgujeong Rodeo Street
압구정 로데오 거리

Gangnam-gu, Apgujeong-ro 46-gil 30
서울 강남구 압구정로 46길 30

It was the center of fashion in the early 90s and was the stomping ground for the younger generation who wanted to break away from the order and the values of the older generation. In the past, it was famous for the children of rich families driving imported cars and wearing high-end brand clothes, similar to Beverly Hills Rodeo Street, but now it has developed into a place representing various youth cultures and high-tech trends. Here, you can find luxury brand stores, private label clothing stores, and shoe stores. Also, dermatology, plastic surgery, and hair shops are abundant. It also has many restaurants and attractions that have spread through word of mouth among young people, so there are many options to please your palate.

16 min walk, **838m**
from **EXIT #2**

Each store has own business hours.

(336) APGUJEONG 압구정

Sinsadong Garosu-gil
신사동 가로수길

Gangnam-gu, Apgujeong-ro 126
서울 강남구 압구정로 126

Garosu-gil has been the hottest neighborhood in Seoul in recent years. It was once a place where galleries and designer shops were concentrated. At one time, movie companies came in one after another, as well as painting dealers. So there are many old stores in between the alleys. Of course, various fashion road shops are the trend now. If you have a favorite shop while taking a walk, you can go in and look around for a while. You can find pretty cafes and restaurants as well.

12 min walk, 553m
from EXIT #5

Each store has own business hours.

(339)=(734)=(923) EXPRESS BUS TERMINAL 고속터미널

Goto Mall (Gangnam Terminal Underground Shopping Complex)
고투몰

Seocho-gu, Shinbanpo-ro 200
서울 서초구 신반포로 200

Goto Mall is Gangnam's largest underground shopping mall, located in the basement of the Gangnam Express Bus Terminal. It sells a variety of items that surpass department stores, such as clothing, cosmetics, accessories, interior accessories, handicrafts, and flowers. Around Gangnam Express Terminal Station, cultural and accommodation facilities such as Shinsegae Department Store, Shinsegae Central City, JW Marriott Hotel, and Seoul Arts Center are located. Shopping is possible regardless of the weather, and the subway is connected, making it easy to move anywhere.

3 min walk, 140m
from EXIT #8-1

Everyday 10 a.m. - 10 p.m.

gotomall.kr

Sebit Seom (Floating Island)
세빛섬

Seocho-gu, Ollimpik-daero 2085-14
서울 서초구 올림픽대로 2085-14

Sebit Seom (Floating Island), which lights up the Han River beautifully, consists of a total of four artificial islands with wedding conventions, Italian restaurants, buffets, and cafes and is used as a space for yachts, tubesters, and various exhibitions, performances, and events to enjoy. Boasting a fantastic night view where colorful and beautiful LED lights harmonize with the Han River, it is one of Seoul's most visited night spots and a filming location for various dramas and movies. Don't forget to take photos at various "photo spots," such as FIC conventions, outdoor decks, and rooftop observatories.

24 min walk, 1.3km
from EXIT #8-1

Each store has own business hours.

www.somesevit.co.kr

Central City
센트럴 시티

Seocho-gu, Shinbanpo-ro 176
서울 서초구 신반포로 176

It is a mega-complex with JW Marriot hotel, express bus terminal, subway lines no. 3, 7, 9, Shinsegae department store, Megabox cinema, a bookstore, and Famille Station that features numerous restaurants to choose from. It's one of the busiest spots in Seoul, but it also means a lot of things to do and see. Underground stores are the go-to place to find sweet deals and steals.

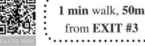

1 min walk, **50m** from **EXIT #3**

Google Maps

Famille Station (Restaurants) 10 a.m. - 10 p.m.
Express Bus Terminal 5 a.m. - 1 a.m.
Shinsegae Department Store 10 a.m. - 8 p.m.
Megabox (Cinema) 7 a.m. - 3 a.m.

www.shinsegaecentralcity.com

Bukchon Hanok Village
북촌 한옥마을

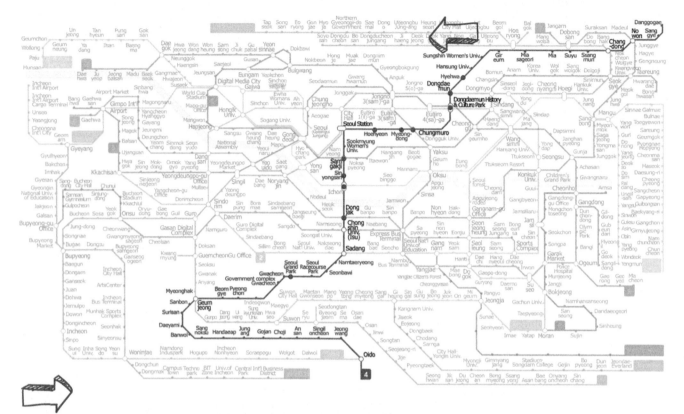

(420) HYEHWA 혜화

- Marronnier Park
  마로니에공원

(421)=(128) DONGDAEMUN 동대문

- Heunginjimun Park 흥인지문 공원
- Dongdaemun/Heunginjimun Gate 동대문/흥인지문
- Cheonggyecheon 청계천

(423)=(331) CHUNGMURO 충무로

- Namsangol Hanok Village
  남산골 한옥 마을

(424) MYEONGDONG 명동

- Myeongdong 명동
- Myeongdong Catholic Cathedral
  명동 성당
- Namsan Seoul Tower
  Cable Car Ticket Booth
  남산 서울타워 케이블카 매표소

(425) HOEHYEON 회현

- Namdaemun Market 남대문 시장
- Namdaemun Gate 남대문

(428)=(628) SAMGAKJI 삼각지

- War Memorial 전쟁기념관

(429) SINYONGSAN 신용산

- Amore Pacific Museum of Art
  아모레퍼시픽미술관

(430) ICHON 이촌

- The National Museum of Korea 국립중앙박물관

(431)=(920) DONGJAK 동작

- National Cemetery 국립 서울 현충원

(437) SEOUL GRAND PARK 대공원

- Seoul Grand Park 서울대공원

- **This line connects north and south Seoul**
- **Number of stations: 48**
- **Termini : Danggogae / Oido**

46

(420) HYEHWA 혜화

Marronnier Park
마로니에공원

Jongno-gu Daehak-ro 104
서울 종로구 대학로 104

Located on Daehangno (College Street), it is always full of energy and inspiration. It can get quite crowded on the weekends. Named after its symbolic marronnier (horse chestnut) tree, it is home to a variety of outdoor cultural event centers, exhibitions, and art centers (hence more famously known as the "Mecca of plays"), which all began to develop in 1975 when Seoul National University relocated away from this site. Since then, small theaters and cafes have flourished, making it a popular place for meetings and relaxation. Bands, singers, dance groups, and comedians show off their talents.

 1 min walk, **93m** from **EXIT #2**

Google Maps

OPEN 24 HRS

(421)=(128) DONGDAEMUN 동대문

Heunginjimun Park
흥인지문 공원

4 min walk, 235m from EXIT #1

Dongdaemun/Heunginjimun Gate
동대문/흥인지문

4 min walk, 235m from EXIT #1

Cheonggyecheon
청계천

3 min walk, 155m from EXIT #6

This place is already introduced in the previous pages.

(423)=(331) CHUNGMURO 충무로

Namsangol Hanok Village
남산골 한옥 마을

6 min walk, 306m from EXIT #4

This place is already introduced in the previous pages.

Myeongdong
명동

Jung-gu, Myeongdong 8-gil 52
서울 중구 명동8길 52

Myeongdong, which attracts about 2 million people every day, is considered the "No. 1 tourist destination in Korea" and can be called a "shopper's heaven." You can find a variety of items that are difficult to find, from high-end brands to cosmetics and souvenirs. Thanks to this, it has long become an essential course for foreign travelers visiting Seoul. Most stores have foreign language-speaking staff. One day might not be enough to look around Myeongdong shopping streets, which include large shopping malls, high-rise department stores, restaurants and cafes, and street vendors. This is why many shoppers visit this place more than once. During the day, traffic is restricted to tourists and pedestrians, so you can look around comfortably. There is a shopping mall as good as Myeongdong in nearby Dongdaemun, so it would be better to visit it together.

6 min walk, **231m** from **EXIT #6**

Google Maps

Each store has own business hours.

Myeongdong Catholic Cathedral
명동 성당

Jung-gu, Myeongdong-gil 74
서울 중구 명동길 74

Located in downtown Seoul, it is the birthplace of the Roman Catholic Church community in Korea. The main building stands at 23m high, and the steeple goes as high as 45m. With Emperor Gojong's ceremony of laying the first stone, it was constructed in 1892 with 20 different types of red and gray bricks that were locally fired. It cost around $60,000 USD, which was supported by the Paris Foreign Missions Society. English mass is available every Sunday at 9 a.m.

9 min walk, **427m** from **EXIT #10**

Google Maps

Check website for church schedule.

www.mdsd.or.kr

Namsan Seoul Tower
Cable Car Ticket Booth
남산 서울타워 케이블카 매표소

Jung-gu, Sopa-ro 83
서울 중구 소파로 83

It has established itself as a "Romantic Island" in the city center. It is a 236.7m-high tower located at the top of Namsan Mountain (262m), which has long been widely known as a place for everlasting romance. It boasts the best view of Seoul from 480m above sea level. It is a symbol of Seoul, which has been ranked as the No. 1 tourist attraction chosen by foreigners and a "sacred place" for couples around the world who dream of eternal love. "Locks of Love" and "Heart Chair" for couples are very popular. Also, make sure to check out the highest toilet in Seoul, which is located on the second floor of the observatory.

13 min walk, **509m** from **EXIT #3**

Google Maps

Everyday 10 a.m. - 11 p.m.

www.cablecar.co.kr

Namdaemun Market
남대문 시장

Jung-gu, Namdaemunshijang 4-gil 21
서울 중구 남대문시장4길 21

It is the largest traditional market in Korea and a huge distribution space visited by 500,000 people a day. It has been playing the role of downtown since the mid-Joseon Dynasty and has a wide range of products like its long history. You can find all kinds of adult clothing at places like Queen Plaza and Jangti Moa. Children's clothing stores are large enough to account for 80% of the nation's children's clothing market. In addition, there are shops selling kitchenware, agricultural and marine products, everyday commodities, and imported products. Most of the products traded here are manufactured, produced, and sold by merchants. The restaurants in alleys that have been with the history of the market are also famous, with the most famous menu being braised cutlassfish. There are lots to see, eat, and enjoy.

2 min walk, **116m** from **EXIT #5**

Google Maps

Each store has own business hours.

www.namdaemunmarket.co.kr

Namdaemun Gate
남대문

Jung-gu, Sejong-daero 40
서울 중구 세종대로 40

Officially known as the Sungnyemun, it is Korea's national treasure No. 1 and is one of the 8 Gates in the Fortress Wall from the Joseon Dynasty that surrounded the city of Seoul. It was first built in the last year of King Taejo in 1398 and rebuilt in 1447. The most notable difference of this gate is the tablet that has its name written vertically, while other gates have them horizontally. The wooden pagoda gate at the top was destroyed by fire in 2008 and was restored in 2013. It is a majestic gate in the middle of Seoul that is worth a quick stop, especially if you are in the Myeong-dong or Namdaemun market area.

10 min walk, **363m** from **EXIT #5**

Google Maps

OPEN 24 HRS

War Memorial
전쟁기념관

Yongsan-gu, Itaewon-ro 29
서울 용산구 이태원로 29

It was constructed by the War Memorial Service Korea Society in 1994 To commemorate the sacrifice of the fallen heroes of the Korean War (1950-1953). This large-scale museum houses over 33,000 artifacts, and about 10,000 of those are on display throughout its five indoor and outdoor halls – Expeditionary Forces Room, Patriotic Memorial Room, War History Room, 6.25 Korean War Room, Development Hall, and Large Machinery Room. It's a superbly thought-out massive museum with amazing exhibitions that reconstruct the most tragic yet prominent chapter of Korean history. All this for free.

4 min walk, **262m** from **EXIT #12**

Google Maps

Everyday 9:30 a.m. - 6 p.m. Closed on Monday (If a national holiday falls on a Monday, it's closed the following day)

www.warmemo.or.kr

(429) SINYONGSAN 신용산

Amore Pacific Museum of Art
아모레퍼시픽미술관

Yongsan-gu Hangang-daero 100
서울 용산구 한강대로 100

The Amore Pacific Museum of Art is a newly opened art museum at Amore Pacific's new headquarter in Yongsan, which aims to become an "open space to discover beauty in everyday life" and to communicate with the public. In the exhibition room on the first basement floor, a variety of planned exhibitions are held, encompassing antique, contemporary art, and Korean art. On the first floor of the spacious "Atrium," which extends from the first to third floors above the ground, there is an art museum lobby, a museum shop, an exhibition space "APMA cabinet," and an exhibition library (apLAP).

2 min walk, **84m**
from **EXIT #2**

Everyday 10 a.m. - 6 p.m.
(Last admission 5:30 p.m.)
Closed on Monday

apma.amorepacific.com

(430) ICHON 이촌

The National Museum of Korea
국립중앙박물관

Yongsan-gu, Seobinggo-ro 137
서울 용산구 서빙고로 137

The National Museum of Korea, where the essence of Korean history and culture lives, is Korea's most beloved treasure trove. Through exhibitions and education, it tells the story of 420,000 collections with thousands of years of history, ranging from the simple hand axes of the Paleolithic era to the colorful gold crown of the Three Kingdoms period, celadon of the Goryeo Dynasty, paintings of the Joseon Dynasty, modern photographs, and world cultural centers. It provides realistic digital videos and VR experiences for a more vivid experience. Spending a day at the National Museum of Korea will be a special experience.

3 min walk, **308m**
from **EXIT #2**

M/T/TH/F/SU - 10 a.m. - 6 p.m.
(Last admission 5:30 p.m.)
W/SA - 10 a.m. - 9 p.m.
(Last admission 8:30 p.m.)

www.museum.go.kr

(431)=(920) DONGJAK 동작

National Cemetery
국립 서울 현충원

Dongjak-gu Hyeonchung-ro 210
서울 동작구 현충로 210

One hundred four thousand soldiers died during the Korean War, but many of their bodies were never found, along with the remains of some 7,000 unknown soldiers whose bodies were found. The remains of more than 54,000 martyred patriots have been buried in the Burial Plots, which are divided into various sections: graves of soldiers, police officers, meritorious citizens, and key figures of the provisional government. Every year on June 6th (Memorial Day), memorial services and events are held at the Seoul National Cemetery to honor these brave patriots. It's a flawlessly kept cemetery with amazing scenery. It's not only great for a history lesson but also wonderful for a leisurely walk. It is extremely crowded on June 6th, Memorial Day in Korea.

1 min walk, **62m**
from **EXIT #8**

Everyday 6 a.m. - 6 p.m.

www.snmb.mil.kr

(437) SEOUL GRAND PARK 대공원

Seoul Grand Park
서울대공원

Gwacheon-si Daegongwongwangjang-ro 102
경기 과천시 대공원광장로 102

It is Korea's first zoo, created by the Japanese occupying forces in 1909 when built in the middle of the former royal palace, Changgyeonggung. It was relocated to its current location in 1984. It is now home to nearly 3,000 animals and 350 species from all around the globe, making it the 10th largest in the world. Facilities include hills, hiking trails, Seoul Grand Park Zoo, Children's Zoo, Rose Garden, Seoul Land Museum Park, and the Seoul Museum of Modern Art. Make sure to bring comfortable shoes, as it could take you the whole day to see the place.

10 min walk, 405m
from **EXIT #2**

NAVER MAP   Google Maps

Everyday 9 a.m. - 6 p.m.

grandpark.seoul.go.kr

Namdaemun Gate
남대문

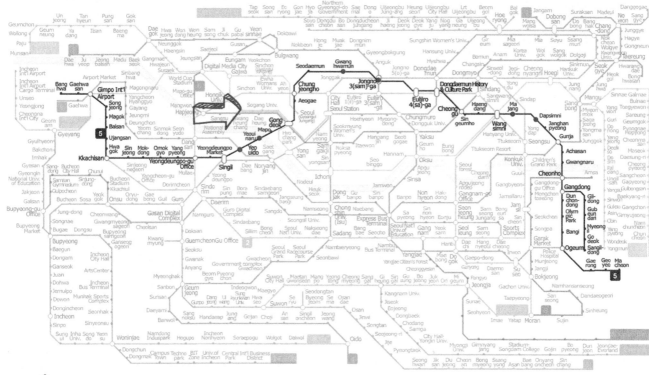

(525)=(915) YEOUIDO 여의도

- IFC Mall IFC 몰
- Yeouido Park 여의도공원

(527) YEOUINARU 여의나루

- 63 Square 63 스퀘어

(533) GWANGHWAMUN 광화문

- Gwanghwamun Square 광화문광장
- Mugyodong Nakji (Octopus) 무교동 낙지
- Seoul History Museum 서울역사박물관
- Sejong Center for the Performing Arts 세종문화회관

(534)=(329)=(130) JONGNO 3(SAM)-GA 종로3가

- Tapgol Park 탑골공원
- Jongmyo Royal Shrine 종묘
- Nagwon Instrument Arcade 낙원악기상가

(541) MAJANG 마장

- Majangdong Meat Alley 마장동 고기 골목

(542) DAPSIMNI 답십리

- Dapsimni Antique Art Street
  답십리 고미술 상가

- **This is a long line crossing from the west to the east of Seoul, crossing the Han River**
- **3rd longest underground tunnel in the world (52.3km)**
- **Number of stations: 51**
- **Termini : Banghwa Sangil-dong / Macheon**

---

(525)=(915) YEOUIDO 여의도

IFC Mall
IFC 몰

Yeongdeungpo-gu Gukjegeumyung-ro 10
서울 영등포구 국제금융로 10

Claiming to be an "entirely new international standard mall," it is a 17m-high building composed of glass pavilions, where you can enjoy modern and spacious corridors with abundant natural lighting. It has many global fashion brands, such as GAP, Guess, Giordano, H&M, Hollister, and Lacoste, as well as local brands. It also has a great selection of restaurants and entertainment facilities. It's a modern and futuristic mall worth visiting. The complex is connected to the Conrad Hotel.

6 min walk, 328m
from **EXIT #3**

Everyday 10 a.m. - 10 p.m.

ifcmallseoul.com

Yeouido Park
여의도공원

Yeongdeungpo-gu Yeouigongwon-ro 68
서울 영등포구 여의공원로 68

It is a huge recreational park located in the center of Seoul, which was originally an asphalt-covered place frequented by roller skaters and bicyclists. After its construction in 1997, which took two years, it finally opened in 1999 and became a Seoul citizen's favorite spot. It is known for beautiful cherry blossoms during the Spring, and an annual fireworks show taking place in October. It is a beautiful park on the riverside. Best to come with an empty stomach as there is an endless number of restaurants to choose from. It can be extremely crowded during cherry blossom season.

11 min walk, 354m
from **EXIT #3**

OPEN 24 HRS

www.ydp.go.kr

(527) YEOUINARU 여의나루

63 Square
63 스퀘어

Yeongdeungpo-gu 63-ro 50
서울 영등포구 63로 50

Standing at 250m (819ft) high, it is the tallest gold-clad structure in the world and was the tallest building in Korea until 2003. It was built as a landmark for the 1988 Seoul Summer Olympics. It provides magnificent views of the Han River and mountains. Its facilities include restaurants, an art gallery, a shopping mall, and an aquarium. If you can shell out some cash for a romantic date night, this is the place to go.

They even have an elevator dedicated specifically for couples, which gives you an exclusive 80-second ride in it (as part of a special package you purchase).

17 min walk, 1.1km
from **EXIT #4**

Everyday
Aquarium 10 a.m. - 7 p.m.
(Last admission 6:30 p.m.)
Art Exhbit Hall 10 a.m. - 8:30 p.m.
(Last admission 8 p.m.)

www.63art.co.kr

Gwanghwamun Square
광화문광장

Jongno-gu, Sejong-daero 175
서울 종로구 세종대로 175

During the Joseon Dynasty, the Gwanghwamun Gate was the main gate of Gyeongbokgung Palace. In 2009, a huge square was built here, reaching all the way to Cheonggye Plaza, and it became a must-see attraction for citizens as well as foreign tourists. You can see huge statues of Korea's most beloved historical figures. The statue of King Sejong, who created Hangul, is located and serves as the center of the square. The statue of Admiral Yi Sun-shin, who saved the country from Japanese aggression, is also loved by citizens. You can also find the mythical creature Haechi, which is the symbol of the city. Artificial ponds and fountains cool down citizens in summer. Behind the statue of King Sejong, there is an entrance to the exhibition hall in the underground space, which commemorates the King's life as well as the story of Admiral Yi Suin Sin.

5 min walk, 233m
from **EXIT #2**

Google Maps

OPEN 24 HRS

gwanghwamun.seoul.go.kr/main.do

Mugyodong Nakji (Octopus)
무교동 낙지

Jongno-gu, Jongro-3-gil 30
서울 종로구 종로3길 30

It is chopped baby octopus marinated in gochujang (hot chili pepper sauce) and stir-fried with vegetables such as onions, scallions, cabbage, and carrots. It is most notorious for its spiciness coming from gochujang sauce, but its nutritional benefits completely offset it. It usually gets an equal amount of likes and dislikes, but if you are a fan of spicy food, you should definitely try (and cry).

4 min walk, 290m
from **EXIT #3**

Google Maps

Everyday 10 a.m. - 10 p.m.

Seoul History Museum
서울역사박물관

Jongno-gu, Saemunan-ro 55
서울 종로구 새문안로 55

In 2002, the Seoul History Museum opened on the site of Gyeonghui Palace to show the history and culture of Seoul from prehistoric times to modern times. The space and exhibition are composed of an open system, centered in the yard away from the existing room, and are experience-oriented. It operates a Touch Museum Corner where you can see video information about the relics while touching them. The exhibitions help to understand Seoul by organizing and showing the history and traditional culture of Seoul. It has become a cultural center of Seoul, providing opportunities for Seoul citizens and foreign visitors to feel and experience the culture of Seoul.

7 min walk, 461m
from **EXIT #7**

Google Maps

Everyday 9 a.m. - 6 p.m.
Closed on Monday (If a national holiday falls on a Monday, it's closed the following day).

museum.seoul.go.kr/eng/index.do

(533) GWANGHWAMUN 광화문

Sejong Center for the Performing Arts
세종문화회관

Jongno-gu, Sejong-daero 175
서울 종로구 세종대로 175

It was established by the Seoul Metropolitan Government and is a representative cultural and artistic institution in Seoul. It was the gateway to Korean performing arts and the only channel for international performing arts. It was recognized as one of the world's leading venues of performing arts and served as the cradle of Korean fine arts in the 70s and 80s. Following the remodeling of Sejong Grand Theater, Sejong Chamber Hall, Sejong M Theater, Art Building Extension, Sejong Art Museum, and Sejong S Theater have been reorganized, and they are serving as Seoul's cultural and artistic hub through various cultural events. Visit the homepage for event information.

2 min walk, 119m from **EXIT #1**

Google Maps

Visit home page for event schedule

www.sejongpac.or.kr

(534)(=329)=(130) JONGNO 3(SAM)-GA 종로3가

Tapgol Park
탑골공원

5 min walk, 338m from EXIT #1

Jongmyo Royal Shrine
종묘

3 min walk, 299m from Exit #11

Nagwon Instrument Arcade
낙원악기상가

2 min walk, 146m from EXIT #5

These places are already introduced in the previous pages.

(541) MAJANG 마장

Majangdong Meat Alley
마장동 고기 골목

Seongdong-gu, Majang-ro 35-gil 68
서울 성동구 마장로35길 68

Equipped with modern and clean facilities, it is the largest meat market in Korea. You can buy fresh meat arriving every hour. They come from many different parts of Korea and overseas. You can usually buy high-quality meats for up to 30% cheaper than you would pay at a supermarket. Many of the shops also have dining areas attached to them, and you can enjoy fresh meats right on site. You can get fresh Korean beef at a discounted price. Don't expect it to be a fancy Korean BBQ restaurant, though.

16 min walk, 826m from **EXIT #2**

Google Maps

Each store has own business hours but most open in the morning.

(542) DAPSIMNI 답십리

Dapsimni Antique Art Street
답십리 고미술 상가

Dongdaemun-gu, Gomisul-ro 39
서울 동대문구 고미술로 39

Antiquities occupy the streets, from stone statues that are two to three times the height of a person to palm-sized ornaments. There are also various types of other items, ranging from fairly large old furniture, door handles, and Buddha statues to household goods such as inkstones, millstones, furnaces, and brass bowls. When you enter a store, the density also deepens. You can also find antique accessories such as traditional Korean ornamental hairpins. Recently, the proportion of antique products from China and Southeast Asia has increased. Western antiques are often seen. Prices range from several thousand won to several million won.

1 min walk, **97m** from **EXIT #2**

Everyday 9:30 a.m. - 7 p.m.
Closed on Sunday

Gwanghwamun Square
광화문광장

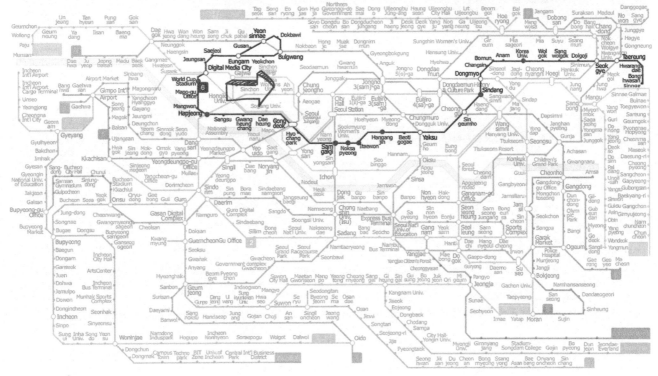

(619) WORLD CUP STADIUM 월드컵 경기장

- Seoul World Cup Stadium
  서울 월드컵 경기장
- World Cup Park
  월드컵 공원

(622)=(238) HAPJEONG 합정

- Yanghwajin Foreign Missionary Cemetery
  양화진외국인선교사묘원
- Jeoldusan Martyrs' Shrine
  절두산 성지
- Mecenatpolis Mall
  메세나폴리스몰

(628)=(428) SAMGAKJI 삼각지

- War Memorial
  전쟁기념관

(629) NOKSAPYEONG 녹사평

- Gyeongridan-gil Road
  경리단길

(630) ITAEWON 이태원

- Itaewon Special Tourist Zone
  이태원 관광 특구

(631) HANGANGJIN 한강진

- Namsan Botanical Garden
  남산 야외 식물원

(635)=(206) SINDANG 신당

- Hwanghak-dong Flea Market
  황학동 벼룩시장
- Chungmu Art Center
  충무 아트센터
- Sindangdong Tteokbokki Town
  신당동 떡볶이타운

(640) KOREA UNIVERSITY 고려대학교

- Yeonghwiwon & Sunginwon
  Royal Tombs 영휘원과 숭인원
- King Sejong the Great Memorial Hall
  세종대왕기념관

- **This is a U-shaped line**
- **When a train arrives at Eungam, it runs through what is the "Eungam Loop," a one-way loop of stations, then it continues to Sinnae.**
- **Number of stations: 38**
- **Termini : Eungam / Sinnae**

(619) WORLD CUP STADIUM 월드컵 경기장

Seoul World Cup Stadium
서울 월드컵 경기장

Mapo-gu, Seongsan-dong 515-39
서울 마포구 성산동 515-39

Constructed as the main stadium for the 2002 FIFA World Cup Korea/Japan, it is the largest football-only stadium in Asia, with a capacity of 66,704 seats. The roof was designed to resemble the shape of a traditional Korean kite, and it covers 90% of the seats. There are five theme parks around the stadium, surrounded by trees and fountains, and they are just great for a stroll, both in the morning and evening. When the biggest rivals in the K-League (FC Seoul & Suwon Bluewings) collide at the stadium, you should consider joining the crowd.

World Cup Park
월드컵 공원

Mapo-gu, Haneulgongwon-ro 86
서울 마포구 하늘공원로 86

Nanjido Island, where the park is located, was a landfill site from 1978-93. However, as the huge artificial mountain was demolished and an ecological park was created, it has now been reborn as a beloved park for Seoul citizens in commemoration of the FIFA 2022 Korea/Japan World Cup. It has five theme parks, including Pyeonghwa (Peace) Park, Haneul (Sky) Park, Noeul (Sunset) Park, Nanjicheon Park, and Nanji Hangang Park. Currently, 733,000 trees of 92 species fill the park, and Nanji Pond and Nanjicheon Stream are added to create beautiful natural scenery. The Exhibition Hall, where you can see the overall history and transformation of Nanjido Island, and Nanji Pond, where you can see species of animals and plants and various birds, are famous places in the park. Now, even on days when there are no soccer games, it is loved as a walking trail for citizens, and various learning programs and events are also provided.

Yanghwajin Foreign Missionary Cemetery
양화진외국인선교사묘원

5 min walk, 320m from EXIT #7

Jeoldusan Martyrs' Shrine
절두산 성지

7 min walk, 482m from EXIT #7

Mecenatpolis Mall
메세나폴리스몰

1 min walk, 35m from EXIT #10

These places are already introduced in the previous pages.

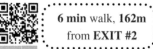

6 min walk, **162m** from **EXIT #2**

Google Maps

Check event schedule for hours.

www.sisul.or.kropen_content/worldcup

15 min walk, **528m** from **EXIT #1**

Google Maps

OPEN 24 HRS parks.seoul.go.krtemplate/sub/worldcuppark.do

(628)=(428) SAMGAKJI 삼각지

War Memorial
전쟁기념관

4 min walk, 262m from EXIT #12

This place is already introduced in the previous pages.

(629) NOKSAPYEONG 녹사평

Gyeongridan-gil Road
경리단길

Yongsan-gu, Noksapyeong-daero 234
서울 용산구 녹사평대로 234

It is one of the most popular streets in Itaewon. When you walk from Exit 2 of Noksapyeong Station and climb up the hill, you can find small restaurants, cafes, and pubs lined up throughout the alleys that spread like spider webs around the wide street. Unique shops on the alleys played a crucial role in creating the current Gyeongridan-gil, and as a result, a commercial district was formed around alleys, not on the roadside. It has rapidly emerged as a trendy place among young people who are tired of franchise cafes and restaurants. There are a handful of unique craft beer pubs. There seem to be more restaurants and craft beer pubs run by foreigners than Koreans.

7 min walk, **385m** from **EXIT 2**

Each store has own business hours.

(630) ITAEWON 이태원

Itaewon Special Tourist Zone
이태원 관광 특구

Yongsan-gu, Itaewon-ro 150
서울 용산구 이태원로 150

Itaewon is the first special tourist zone in Seoul and is a multinational and multicultural area inhabited by more than 20,000 foreigners. More than 2,000 stores, including accommodation facilities, restaurants, entertainment facilities, and travel agencies, are concentrated in alleys. Antique Furniture Street, which has more than 100 stores from Hamilton Hotel to Bogwang-ro, is also famous. In addition, you can experience exotic culture and food at World Food Street, which is filled with restaurants from more than 40 countries run by foreigners. Various performances and events are held every October, and the Itaewon Global Village Festival is especially famous. US dollars and yen are freely used, and it is easy to do business with merchants in languages such as English, Japanese, and Chinese. It is the most exotic place in Korea.

4 min walk, **282m** from **EXIT #4**

Google Maps

Each store has own business hours.

www.itaewon.or.kr

(631) HANGANGJIN 한강진

Namsan Botanical Garden
남산 야외 식물원

Yongsan-gu, Itaewon-dong 259-16
서울 용산구 이태원동 259-16

It is an outdoor botanical garden located in Namsan Urban Nature Park in Yongsan-gu, Seoul. It's divided into a pond, an aquatic botanical garden, a pine-tree complex featuring pine trees from all eight provinces of Korea, a wildflower garden. Admission is free. In the middle, there is an "infant forest experience center" where children can play. There is a path of acupressure on the way to the pine-tree complex after passing through the moss garden. In spring and autumn, many flowers bloom in the wild garden and you can see a beautiful appearance. You can't see flowers from June to August.

23 min walk, **1.3km** from **EXIT #1**

Google Maps

OPEN 24 HRS

(635)=(206) SINDANG 신당

Hwanghak-dong Flea Market
황학동 벼룩시장

6 min walk, 392m from EXIT #1

Chungmu Art Center
충무 아트센터

2 min walk, 105m from EXIT #9

Sindangdong Tteokbokki Town
신당동 떡볶이타운

4 min walk, 236m from EXIT #8

These places are already introduced in the previous pages.

(640) KOREA UNIVERSITY 고려대학교

Yeonghwiwon & Sunginwon Royal Tombs 영휘원과 숭인원

Dongdaemun-gu Hongreung-ro 90
서울 동대문구 홍릉로 90

Yeonghwiwon is the tomb of Queen Sunheon, the concubine of Emperor Gojong of the Korean Empire, and Sunginwon is the tomb of Yi Jin-won, the first son of Prince Uimin, the last crown prince of the Korean Empire. Walking along the park away from the busy city is a healing relaxation that transcends time and space.

17 min walk, **824m** from **EXIT #3**

Google Maps

Everyday 9 a.m. - 6 p.m.
Closed on Monday

King Sejong the Great
Memorial Hall 세종대왕기념관

Dongdaemun-gu Hoegi-ro 56
서울 동대문구 회기로 56

Established to honor King Sejong the Great, who is considered to be one of the greatest Kings in Korean history for his saintly virtues and brilliant achievements. It is a 3-story building that houses an exhibition area (Hangul, Science, Traditional Music, Art, and Outdoor), an auditorium, a laboratory, and a reference room. If you have ever wondered why he is revered as the greatest king throughout Korean history, you will be nodding your head as you learn more about him at this great museum.

15 min walk, 648m
from **EXIT #4**

Google Maps

Everyday 9 a.m. - 6 p.m. (Mar - Oct)
9 a.m. - 5:30 p.m. (Nov - Feb)
Closed on Monday

sejongkorea.org

Sindangdong Tteokbokki Town
신당동 떡볶이타운

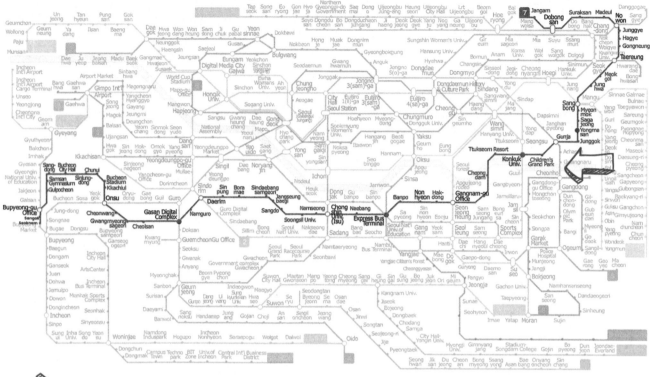

(723) YONGMASA 용마산

- Mt. Yongmasan
  용마산

(727)=(212) KONKUK UNIV. 건대입구

- Common Ground
  커먼그라운드

(734)=(923)=(339) EXPRESS BUS TERMINAL 고속터미널

- Goto Mall (Gangnam Terminal Underground Shopping Complex) 고투몰
- Sebit Seom (Floating Island) 세빛섬
- Central City 센트럴 시티

(746) GASAN DIGITAL COMPLEX가산디지털단지

- Gasan Digital Complex Outlet Town
  가산디지털단지 아울렛타운

- **This line connects north and south Seoul but does not run through the city center.**
- **Number of stations: 53**
- **Termini : Jangam / Seoknam**

(723) YONGMASA 용마산

Mt. Yongmasan
용마산

Jungnang-gu Myeonmok 4-dong San 75-1
서울특별시 중랑구 면목4동 산75-1

Mt. Yongmasan is 348 meters high, with numerous observation platforms that provide great views of Seoul. Thanks to its friendly altitude, it is suitable for people of all ages. In fact, some go hiking in casual clothing. Make sure to check out the waterfall within the park you meet on your way. It is the largest artificial waterfall in Asia. Its neighbor, Mt. Achasan is standing at just 287 meters high. It also offers a great view of Seoul. If you choose to reach the summits of both mountains, it will take about 2 hours total.

17 min walk, **842m** from **EXIT #2**

Google Maps

OPEN 24 HRS

(727)=(212) KONKUK UNIV. 건대입구

Common Ground
커먼그라운드

3 min walk, 196m from EXIT #6

This place is already introduced in the previous pages.

(734)=(339)=(923) EXPRESS BUS TERMINAL 고속터미널

Goto Mall (Gangnam Terminal Underground Shopping Complex)
고투몰

3 min walk, 140m from EXIT #8-1

Sebit Seom (Floating Island)
세빛섬

24 min walk, 1.3km from EXIT #8-1

Central City
센트럴 시티

1 min walk, 50m from EXIT #3

These places are already introduced in the previous pages.

(746) GASAN DIGITAL COMPLEX
가산디지털단지

Gasan Digital Complex Outlet Town
가산디지털단지 아울렛타운

Geumcheon-gu Beotkkot-ro 266
서울 금천구 벚꽃로 266

This is where clothing companies located in Guro Industrial Complex operated their own permanent stores in the past. With the opening of Mario Outlet in 2001, a large fashion town was formed to become what it is today. After the success of Mario Outlet, large outlets such as W Mall, Fashion Island, and Hansom Factory Outlet have appeared in nearby areas.

There are areas such as Mario Square and Fashion Street, which allow visitors to enjoy shopping while taking a leisurely walk outside.

In addition, large-scale events such as art exhibitions and cooking classes are held there.

It also features a European-style food court.

3 min walk, 309m
from EXIT #4

Google Maps

Everyday
10:30 a.m. - 9 p.m.
(F/SA/SU 9:30 p.m.)

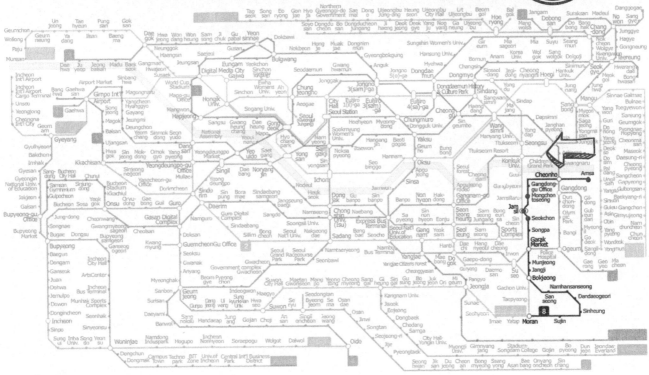

(810) AMSA 암사

- Amsa-dong Prehistoric Settlement Site
  암사동 유적지

(813) MONGCHONTOSEONG 몽촌토성

- Olympic Park
  올림픽공원

(814)=(216) JAMSIL 잠실

- Lotte World
  롯데 월드
- Samjeondobi Stone Monument
  삼전도비

(815)=(933) SEOKCHON 석촌

- Seokchon Lake Park
  석촌호수

- This line has the least number of stations and the shortest route.
- As of 2022, this is one of the two lines (the other being line 9) that does not cross the Han River.
- Number of stations: 18
- Termini : Amsa / Moran

65

(810) AMSA 암사	(813) MONGCHONTOSEONG 몽촌토성	(814)=(216) JAMSIL 잠실

Lotte World
롯데 월드

2 min walk, 143m from EXIT #4

Samjeondobi Stone Monument
삼전도비

6 min walk, 270m from EXIT #3

Amsa-dong Prehistoric Settlement Site 암사동 유적지

Gangdong-gu, Ollimpik-ro 875
서울 강동구 올림픽로 875

This site was excavated in 1925 after a flood washed away the soil on the banks of the Han River, revealing numerous ancient artifacts such as comb-pattern earthenware, stone arrows, and axes. It is established to reproduce the lifestyle of the Neolithic Era (7,000 BC ~ 1,000 BC), with many attractions such as gigantic mud huts, exhibition halls, and promenades. It's a fun and educational place for children and families who want to learn and experience the Neolithic Age.

Olympic Park
올림픽공원

Songpa-gu Ollimpik-ro 424
서울 송파구 올림픽로 424

Originally constructed to host the 1988 Seoul Summer Olympics, this 408-acre park has been transformed into a gigantic recreational park with sports stadiums, forests, and grass. It is divided into several zones - leisure sports park, cultural art park, eco-park, and history experience park. Due to its vast size, it takes many hours (3+) to fully explore the park. For this, you might want to familiarize yourself with the layout of the park before you start. It's an impressive park where modernity and nature coexist in harmony. Ride the Road Train ("Hodori Train") located next to Peace Square to save time.

These places are already introduced in the previous pages.

20 min walk, **1.3km** from **EXIT #4**

Everyday 9:30 a.m. - 6 p.m. Closed on Monday (If a national holiday falls on a Monday, it's closed the following day).

Google Maps

sunsa.gangdong.go.kr

1 min walk, **34m** from **EXIT #1**

OPEN 24 HRS

Google Maps

www.olympicpark.co.kr

Seokchon Lake Park
석촌호수

Songpa-gu Jamsil-ro 148
서울 송파구 잠실로 148

Located inside Songpa NaruPark, it has two artificial lakes, seo-ho (west lake) and dong-ho (east lake), with Songpa-daero running right through them. Seo-ho has Lotte World's "Magic Island" sitting in the middle, while dong-ho is known for its hiking trails and jogging paths laid along its banks. It hosted the "Rubber Duck" sculpture by Dutch artist Florentijn Hofman in 2014. It's a peaceful park conveniently located around the Lotte complex. One of the best places to enjoy cherry blossoms (Apr-May) as it is not as crowded as Yeouido Park.

5 min walk, 458m
from EXIT #8

OPEN 24 HRS

Seokchon Lake Park
석촌호수

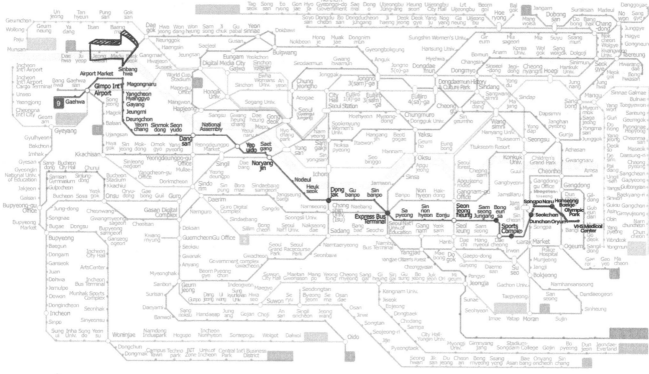

(906) YANGCHEON HYANGGYO 양천향교

- Yangcheon Hyanggyo Confucian School
  양천향교

(912) SEONYUDO 선유도

- Seonyudo Park
  선유도 공원

(914) NATIONAL ASSEMBLY 국회의사당

- National Assembly Building
  국회의사당

(915)=(525) YEOUIDO 여의도

- IFC Mall IFC 몰
- Yeouido Park 여의도공원

(916) SAETGANG 샛강

Yeouido Saetgang Ecological Park 여의도 생태공원

(136)=(917) NORYANGJIN 노량진

- Sayuksinmyo Six Martyrs' Tombs 사육신묘
- Noryangjin Fisheries Market 노량진 수산시장

(920)=(431) DONGJAK 동작

- National Cemetery 국립 서울 현충원

(923)=(734)=(339) EXPRESS BUS TERMINAL 고속터미널

- Goto Mall (Gangnam Terminal Underground Shopping Complex) 고투몰
- Sebit Seom (Floating Island) 세빛섬
- Central City 센트럴 시티

(929) BONGEUNSA 봉은사

- Bongeunsa Temple 봉은사
- COEX 코엑스

(933)=(815) SEOKCHON 석촌

- Seokchon Lake Park 석촌호수

(935) HANSEONG BAEKJE 한성백제

- Seoul (Hanseong) Baekje Museum 한성백제박물관

- **This is the newest addition to the Seoul subway system.**
- **It is often packed back-to-back, especially during rush hour.**
- **Number of stations: 38**
- **Termini : Gaehwa / Sports Complex**

(906) YANGCHEON HYANGGYO 양천향교

Yangcheon Hyanggyo Confucian School 양천향교

Gangseo-gu, Yangcheon-ro 47 Na-gil 53
서울 강서구 양천로47나길 53

Hyanggyo is an educational institution established by the state for the education and edification of local residents by performing rituals to Confucius and various sages. Yangcheonhyanggyo This school was first built in the 11th year of King Taejong (1411) of the Joseon Dynasty, and was fully restored in 1981. The buildings include Daeseongjeon Shrine, a memorial hall, Myeongnyundang Lecture Hall, an auditorium that performs educational functions, Dongjae and Seojae, a dormitory for students, Naesammun Gate, and Oesammun Gate. Inside the Daeseongjeon Shrine, Confucius and his disciples' tablets are enshrined. Now the educational function has disappeared and only the function of ancestral rites remains. Yangcheonhyanggyo Confucian School is the only local Confucian school in Seoul out of 234 local Confucian schools nationwide.

7 min walk, **450m**
from **EXIT #2**

Google Maps

Everyday 10 a.m. - 4 p.m. Closed on Monday

hyanggyo.net

(912) SEONYUDO 선유도

Seonyudo Park 선유도 공원

Yeongdeungpo-gu, Seonyu-ro 343
서울 영등포구 선유로 343

It was a small peak island located in the center of the Han River, has long been loved by artists and poets. However, through Japanese colonial era, the old appearance of Seonyubong Peak disappeared, and from 1978 to 2000, it was used as a water purification plant to supply tap water to the southwestern part of Seoul. In 2002, it has been regenerated as an eco-friendly ecological park that provides leisure, recreation, and education. You can observe the growth and purification process of various aquatic plants that purify water, as well as cultural spaces for recreation such as an amphitheater and educational classes.

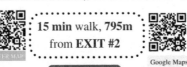

15 min walk, **795m**
from **EXIT #2**

Google Maps

OPEN 24 HRS

www.ydp.go.kr

(914) NATIONAL ASSEMBLY 국회의사당

National Assembly Building 국회의사당

Yeongdeungpo-gu, Euisadang-daero 1
서울 영등포구 의사당대로 1

Located in Yeouido, the National Assembly building symbolizes democracy and human rights in Korea. There is the main building of the National Assembly building, the National Assembly Library on the right, and the National Assembly Hall on the left. You can easily find it from Exits 1 and 6 of the National Assembly Building Station. The library is well-organized. Although there aren't many seats available, there aren't many people, either.

1 min walk, **41m**
from **EXIT #6**

Google Maps

korea.assembly.go.kr

Visitors can make a tour reservation by sending an email to visitor@assembly.go.kr at least 3 days before the planned date.

(915)=(525) YEOUIDO 여의도

IFC Mall
IFC 몰

6 min walk, 328m from EXIT #3

Yeouido Park
여의도공원

11 min walk, 354m from EXIT #3

These places are already introduced in the previous pages.

(916) SAETGANG 샛강

Yeouido Saetgang Ecological Park
여의도 생태공원

Yeongdeungpo-gu Yeouido-dong 49
서울 영등포구 여의도동 49

It is the first ecological park constructed in Korea. It originally opened in 1997 and had a complete renovation project which took place between 2008 and 2011. As a result, it became a massive park with six different themes. It is full of rare species of flora and fauna, such as kestrels, herons, and minnows. It's adjacent to Yeouido Park but has a different ambiance - you can feel nature more and less crowded.

6 min walk, 647m from EXIT #4

OPEN 24 HRS

www.ydp.go.kr

(917)=(136) NORYANGJIN 노량진

Sayuksinmyo Six Martyrs' Tombs
사육신묘

14 min walk, 697m from EXIT #2

Noryangjin Fisheries Market
노량진 수산시장

4 min walk, 248m from EXIT #1

These places are already introduced in the previous pages.

(920)=(431) DONGJAK 동작

National Cemetery
국립 서울 현충원

1 min walk, 62m from EXIT #4

> This place is already introduced in the previous pages.

(923)=(734)=(339) EXPRESS BUS TERMINAL 고속터미널

Goto Mall (Gangnam Terminal Underground Shopping Complex)
고투몰

3 min walk, 140m from EXIT #8-1

Sebit Seom (Floating Island)
세빛섬

24 min walk, 1.3km from EXIT #8-1

Central City
센트럴 시티

1 min walk, 50m from EXIT #3

> These places are already introduced in the previous pages.

(929) BONGEUNSA 봉은사

Bongeunsa Temple
봉은사

Gangnam-gu Bongeunsa-ro 531
서울 강남구 봉은사로 531

This 1,200-year-old temple was originally named Gyeonseongsa temple and was constructed in 794 during the Silla Kingdom (57 BC – 935 AD). After surviving the Joseon Dynasty's suppression of Buddhism, it became the main temple of the Korean Seon (Zen) sect of Buddhism from 1551 to 1936. It is also a famous tourist spot with its "Temple Stay Program," in which visitors can live the life of a monk for a few hours - every Thursday from 2 to 4 p.m., the temple life program is available for foreign visitors. It includes a temple tour, lotus lantern making, Dado (tea-drinking ceremony), and a chance to talk with a monk. All activities are conducted in English. With skyscrapers and modern buildings all around, this tranquil Temple creates the most dramatic contrast in Korea that is so inspirational. Visit the homepage for the latest information.

 1 min walk, 135m from **EXIT #1**

NAVER MAP   Google Maps

Everyday 5 a.m. - 10 p.m.

www.bongeunsa.org

(929) BONGEUNSA 봉은사

COEX
코엑스

Gangnam-gu Yeongdong-daero 513
서울 강남구 영동대로 513

Short for "Convention and Exhibition," This colossal complex houses the convention and exhibition center, the Starfield COEX Mall, three luxury hotels, an urban airport terminal where you can check-in and send baggage without having to go to Incheon airport, a multiplex cinema, the COEX Aquarium. The mall is the largest underground mall in Asia and has a vast array of fashion, lifestyle, accessories, and electronic stores, along with a great selection of restaurants and coffee shops. It's a huge and trendy mall that has everything for your entertainment needs.

EXIT #7 is directly connected to the mall

Google Maps

COEX Convention 10 a.m. - 6 p.m.
Starfield COEX Mall 10:30 a.m. - 10 p.m.

www.coex.co.kr

(933)=(815) SEOKCHON 석촌

Seokchon Lake Park
석촌호수

5 min walk, 458m from EXIT #8

This place is already introduced in the previous pages.

(935) HANSEONG BAEKJE 한성백제

Seoul (Hanseong) Baekje Museum
한성백제박물관

Songpa-gu, Wiryeseong-daero 71
서울 송파구 위례성대로 71

It is a city museum established at an ancient historical site in Songpa-gu to preserve the history and remains of Baekje, one of the Three Kingdoms in ancient Korea. It is a place where you can study Baekje relics in the past, as well as the history of other times, in the special exhibition hall, including a 4D video experience. Since it is in the Olympic Park, you can enjoy the park and the museum together. In particular, if you go to the Hansung Baekje Festival in the fall, you can experience various experience facilities at the museum.

7min walk, **438m** from **EXIT #2**

Google Maps

Everyday 9 a.m. - 7 p.m.
(Nov - Feb SA/SU/Holidays 9 a.m. - 6 p.m.)
Closed on Monday

museum.seoul.go.kr

ROYAL EXPERIENCE

A word of caution about station numbers - Use the number only to identify your location because a number that is less or more than another (e.g., 302 & 803) doesn't necessarily mean that one is further in the west or in the east. Each line starts from a different point and has different routes. Do not assume that you'd have to travel in the ascending or descending order of station numbers and check the map for the location of each station before starting a trip.

(132)=(201) CITY HALL 시청

Deoksugung Palace
덕수궁

Jung-gu Sejong-daero 99
서울 중구 세종대로99

- Take the JONGGAK 종각 bound train at line (132) CITY HALL 시청 station.
- Go 2 stations, and get off at (130)=(329) JONGNO 3-GA 종로3가 station.
- Make a transfer to line 3 by walking to the platform.
- Take the ANGUK 안국 bound train.
- Go 2 stations and get off at (328) ANGUK 안국 station. **EXIT 3.**

approx. 28 min

(328) ANGUK 안국

Changdeokgung Palace
창덕궁

Jongno-gu Yulgok-ro 99
서울 종로구 율곡로 99

Changgyeonggung Palace
창경궁

Jongno-gu Changgyeonggung-ro 185
서울 종로구 창경궁로 185

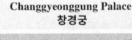

approx. 7 min

- Take the GYEONGBOKGUNG 경복궁 bound train at (328) ANGUK 안국 station.
- Go 1 station and exit at (327) GYEONGBOKGUNG 경복궁 station. **EXIT #5**

(327) GYEONGBOKGUNG 경복궁

Gyeongbokgung Palace
경복궁

Jongno-gu Sajik-ro 161
서울 종로구 사직로 161

Cheongwadae Tour
청와대

Jongno-gu Hyojaro13-gil 45
서울 종로구 효자로13길 45

SPRITUAL GETAWAY

(131) JONGGAK 종각

Jogyesa Temple
조계사

Jongno-gu Ujeongguk-ro 55
서울 종로구 우정국로 55

approx. 16 min

- Take the CITY HALL 시청 bound train at (131) JONGGAK 종각 station.
- Go 1 station and Get off at (132)=(201) CITY HALL 시청. **EXIT #6**

(132)=(201) CITY HALL 시청

Hwangudan Altar
환구단

Jung-gu Sogong-ro 106
서울 중구 소공로 106

approx. 18 min

- Take the SEOUL STATION 서울역 bound train at (132)=(201) CITY HALL 시청 station.
- Go 1 station and get off at (133)=(426) SEOUL STATION 서울역.
- Make a transfer to line 4 by walking to the platform.
- Take the HOEHYEON 회현 bound station.
- Go 2 stations and get off at (424) MYEONGDONG 명동 station. **EXIT #10**

(424) MYEONGDONG 명동

Myeongdong Catholic Cathedral
명동 성당

Jung-gu, Myeongdong-gil 74
서울 중구 명동길 74

approx. 45 min

- Take the HOEHYEON 회현 bound train at (424) MYEONGDONG 명동 station.
- Go 7 stations and get off at (431)=(920) DONGJAK (SEOUL NATIONAL CEMETRY) 동작(현충원) station.
- Make a transfer to line 9 by walking to the platform.
- Take the GUBANPO 구반포 bound train.
- Go 4 more stations and get off at (929) BONGEUNSA 봉은사 station. **EXIT #1**

(929) BONGEUNSA 봉은사

Bongeunsa Temple
봉은사

Gangnam-gu Bongeunsa-ro 531
서울 강남구 봉은사로 531

HIT THE SHOPS

(126)=(211-4) SINSEOLDONG 신설동

Seoul Folk Flea Market
서울풍물시장

Dongdaemun-gu Cheonho-daero 4-gil 21
서울 동대문구 천호대로 4길 21

approx. 24 min

- Take the DONGMYO 동묘앞 bound train at (126)=(211-4) SINSEOLDONG 신설동 station.
- Go 2 stations and get off at (128)=(421) DONGDAEMUN 동대문 station. **EXIT #8**

(128)=(421) DONGDAEMUN 동대문

Dongdaemun Fashion Town
동대문 패션타운

Jung-gu, Jangchungdan-ro 263
서울 중구 장충단로 263

approx. 16 min

- Make a transfer to line 4 by walking to the platform.
- Take the DONGDAEMUN HISTORY & CULTURE PARK 동대문 역사 문화 공원 bound train.
- Go 3 stations and get off at (424) MYEONGDONG station. **EXIT #5**

(424) MYEONGDONG 명동

Myeongdong
명동

Jung-gu, Myeongdong 2-ga
서울 중구 명동2가

approx. 5 min

- Take the OIDO 오이도 bound train at (424) MYEONGDONG 명동 station.
- Go 1 station and get off at (425) HOEHYEON 회현 station. **EXIT #5**

(425) HOEHYEON 회현

Namdaemun Market
남대문 시장

Jung-gu, Namdaemunshijang 4-gil 21
서울 중구 남대문시장4길 21

PAYING RESPECT

(238)=(622) HAPJEONG 합정

**Jeoldusan Martyrs' Shrine
절두산 성지**

Mapo-gu, Tojeong-ro 6
서울 마포구 토정로 6

**Yanghwajin Foreign Missionary
Cemetery 양화진외국인선교사묘원**

Mapo-gu Yanghwajin-gil 46
마포구 양화진길 46

approx. 28 min

- Take the DANGSAN 당산 bound train at (238)=(622) HAPJEONG 합정 station.
- Go 1 station and get off at (237)=(913) DANGSAN 당산 station.
- Make a transfer to line 9 by walking to the platform.
- Take the NATIONAL ASSEMBLY 국회의사당 bound train at (913)=(237).
- Go 4 stations and get off at (917)=(136) NORYANGJIN 노량진 station. **EXIT #2**

(917)=(136) NORYANGJIN 노량진

**Sayuksinmyo Six Martyrs' Tombs
사육신묘**

Dongjak-gu Noryangjin 1-dong
서울 동작구 노량진1동

approx. 24 min

- Take the NODEUL 노들 bound train at (136)=(917) NORYANGJIN 노량진 station.
- Go 3 stations and get off at (920)=(431) DONGJAK 동작 station. **EXIT #8**

(920)=(431) DONGJAK 동작

**National Cemetery
국립 서울 현충원**

Dongjak-gu Hyeonchung-ro 210
서울 동작구 현충로 210

REMEMBERING THE PAST

(326) DONGNIMMUN 독립문

Seodaemun Prison History Hall
서대문 형무소

Seodaemun-gu, Tongil-ro 251
서울 서대문구 통일로 251

Dongnimmun Gate
독립문

Seodaemun-gu Hyeonjeo-dong 941
서울 서대문구 현저동 941

approx. 24 min

- Take the GYEONGBOKGUNG 경복궁 bound train at (326) DONGNIMMUN 독립문 station.
- Go 2 stations and get off at (328) ANGUK 안국 station. **EXIT #4**

(328) ANGUK 안국

National Folk Museum of Korea
국립민속박물관

Jongno-gu, Samcheong-ro 37
서울 종로구 삼청로 37

approx. 40 min

- Take the JONGNO 3(SAM)-GA 종로3가 bound train at (328) ANGUK 안국 station.
- Go 3 stations, and make get off at (331)=(423) CHUNGMURO 충무로 station.
- Make a transfer to line 4 by walking to the platform.
- Take the MYEONGDONG 명동 bound train.
- Go 5 stations and get off at (428)=(628) SAMGAKJI 삼각지 station. **EXIT #1**

(428)=(628) SAMGAKJI 삼각지

War Memorial
전쟁기념관

Yongsan-gu, Itaewon-ro 29
서울 용산구 이태원로 29

approx. 40 min

- Make a transfer to line 6 by walking to the platform.
- Take the NOKSAPYEONG 녹사평 bound train.
- Go 12 stations and get off at (640) KOREA UNIV. 고려대 station. **EXIT #3**

(640) KOREA UNIV. 고려대

King Sejong the Great Memorial Hall
세종대왕 기념관

Dongdaemun-gu Hoegi-ro 57
서울 동대문구 회기로 57

GOING FOR A STROLL

(421)=(128) DONGDAEMUN 동대문

Heunginjimun Park
흥인지문 공원

Jongno-gu Jong-ro 6-ga 70
서울 종로구 종로6가 70

(421)=(128) DONGDAEMUN 동대문

Cheonggyecheon
청계천

Jongno-gu Changsin-dong
서울 종로구 창신동

approx. 22 min

- Take the DONGDAEMUN HISTORY & CULTURE PARK 동대문역사문화공원 bound train at (421)=(128) DONGDAEMUN 동대문 station.
- Go 2 stations and get off at (423)=(331) CHUNGMURO 충무로 station. **EXIT #4**.

(423)=(331) CHUNGMURO 충무로

Namsangol Hanok Village
남산골 한옥 마을

Jung-gu, Toegye-ro 34-gil 28
서울 중구 퇴계로34길 28

approx. 8 min

- Take the DONGGUK UNIV. 동대입구 bound train at (423)=(331) CHUNGMURO 충무로 station.
- Make a transfer to line 3 by walking to the platform.
- Take the OGEUM 오금 bound train.
- Go 5 stations and get off at (336) APGUJEONG 압구정 station. **EXIT #6**.

(336) APGUJEONG 압구정

K-Star Road
케이스타 로드

Gangnam-gu, Apgujeong-ro 394
서울 강남구 압구정동 394

approx. 36 min

- Take the SINSA 신사 bound train at (336) APGUJEONG 압구정 station.
- Go 4 stations and get off at (340)=(223) SEOUL NAT'L UNIV. OF EDUCATION 교대(법원/검찰청) station.
- Make a transfer to line 2 by walking to the platform.
- Take the GANGNAM STATION 강남역 bound train.
- Go 3 stations and get off at (220) SEOLLEUNG 선릉. **EXIT #10**.

(220) SEOLLEUNG 선릉

Seonjeongneung Royal Tombs
서울 선릉과 정릉

Gangnam-gu Samseong-2-dong 100-gil 1
서울 강남구 삼성2동 선릉로100길 1

LET THE EATING BEGIN

(136)=(917) NORYANGJIN 노량진

Noryangjin Fisheries Market
노량진 수산 시장

Dongjak-gu Nodeul-ro 674
서울 동작구 노들로 674

approx. 36 min

- Take the YONGSAN 용산 bound train at (136)=(917) NORYANGJIN 노량진 station.
- Go 7 stations and get off at (129) JONGNO-5(O)-GA 종로5가. **EXIT #8**

(129) JONGNO-5(O)-GA 종로5가

Gwangjang Market
광장시장

Jongno-gu Changgyeonggung-ro 88
서울 종로구 창경궁로 88

approx. 18 min

- Take the JONGNO-3(SAM)-GA 종로3가 bound train at (129) JONGNO-5(O)-GA 종로5가 station.
- Go 1 stations and get off at (130)=(329)=(534) JONGNO-3(SAM)-GA 종로3가.
- Make a transfer to line 3 by walking to the platform.
- Take the EULJIRO-3(SAM)-GA 을지로 3가 bound train.
- Go 7 stations and get off at (332) DONGGUK UNIVERSITY 동대입구역 station. **EXIT #3.**

(332) DONGGUK UNIVERSITY 동대입구역

Jangchung-dong Jokbal (Steamed Pork Trotters)
장충동 족발 골목

Jung-gu, Jangchungdan-ro 174
서울 중구 장충단로 174

approx. 41 min

- Take the YAKSU 약수 bound train at (332) DONGGUK UNIVERSITY 동대입구역 station.
- Go 8 stations and get off at (340)=(223) SEOUL NAT'L UNIV. OF EDUCATION 교대(법원/검찰청) station.
- Make a transfer to line 2 by walking to the platform.
- Take the SEOCHO 서초 bound train.
- Go 7 stations and get off at (230) SILLIN 신림 station. **EXIT #4**

(230) SILLIM 신림

Sillim-dong Sundae Town
신림동 순대타운

Gwanak-gu, Sillim-ro 59-gil 14
서울 관악구 신림로 59길 14

approx. 38 min

- Take the SINDAEBANG 신대방 bound train at (230) SILLIM 신림 station.
- Go 19 stations and get off at (206)=(635) SINDANG 신당 station. **EXIT #8**

(206)=(635) SINDANG 신당

Sindangdong Tteokbokki Town
신당동 떡볶이타운

Jung-gu Cheonggu-ro 77
서울 중구 청구로 77

MODERN TIMES

(536) DONGDAEMUN HISTORY & CULTURE PARK 동대문역사문화공원

Dongdaemun Digital Plaza (DDP)
동대문 디지털 플라자

Jung-gu, Eulji-ro 281
서울 중구 을지로 281

approx. 38 min

- Take the EULJIRO 4(SA)-GA 을지로 4가 bound train at (536) DONGDAEMUN HISTORY & CULTURE PARK 동대문역사문화공원.
- Go 9 stations and get off at (527) YEOUINARU 여의나루 station. **EXIT #4**

(527) YEOUINARU 여의나루

63 Square
63 스퀘어

Yeongdeungpo-gu 63-ro 50
서울 영등포구 63로 50

approx. 5 min

- Take the BANGHWA 방화 bound train at (527) YEOUINARU 여의나루 station.
- Go 2 stations and get off at (525)=(915) YEOUIDO 여의도 station. **EXIT #3**

(525)=(915) YEOUIDO 여의도

IFC Mall
IFC 몰

Yeongdeungpo-gu Gukjegeumyung-ro 10
서울 영등포구 국제금융로 10

approx. 5 min

- Make a transfer to line 9 by walking to the platform.
- Take the SAETGANG 샛강 bound train.
- Go 3 stations and get off at ((923)=(734)=(339) EXPRESS BUS TERMINAL 고속터미널 station. **EXIT #8-1**

(923)=(734)=(339) EXPRESS BUS TERMINAL 고속터미널

Sebit Seom (Floating Island)
세빛섬

Seocho-gu, Ollimpil-daero 2085-14
서울 서초구 올림픽대로 2085-14

		#	ENG	KOR	CHN	TRANSFER	DISTANCE (km)	ACCUM. DISTANCE (km)
		100	Soyosan	소요산	逍遙山		-	0
		101	Dongducheon	동두천	东豆川		2.5	2.5
		102	Bosàn	보산	保山		1.6	4.1
		103	Dongducheon Jungang	동두천중앙	东豆川中央		1.4	5.5
		104	Jihaeng	지행	纸杏		1	6.5
		105	Deokjeong	덕정	德亭		5.6	12.1
		106	Deokgye	덕계	德溪		2.9	15
		107	Yangju	양주	杨州		5.3	20.3
		108	Nogyang	녹양	绿杨		1.6	21.9
		109	Ganeung	가능	佳陵		1.3	23.2
		110	Uijeongbu	의정부	议政府		1.2	24.4
		111	Hoeryong	회룡	回龙		1.6	26
●		112	Mangwolsa	망월사	望月寺		1.4	27.4
●		113	Dobongsan	도봉산	道峰山	⑦	2.3	29.7
●		114	Dobong	도봉	道峰		1.2	30.9
●		115	Banghak	방학	放鹤		1.3	32.2
●		116	Chang-dong	창동	仓洞	④	1.7	33.9
●		117	Nokcheon	녹천	鹿川		1	34.9
●		118	Wolgye	월계	月溪		1.4	36.3
		119	Kwangwoon Univ.	광운대	光云大学		1.1	37.4
●		120	Seokgye	석계	石溪	⑥	1.1	38.5
●		121	Sinimun	신이문	新里门		1.4	39.9
●		122	Hankuk Univ. of Foreign Studies	외대앞	韩国外国语大学		0.8	40.7
		123	Hoegi	회기	回基		0.8	41.5
●	●	124	Cheongnyangni (University of Seoul)	청량리 (서울시립대입구)	清凉里(首尔市立大学)		1.4	42.9
	●	125	Jegidong	제기동	祭基洞		1	43.9
●	●	126	Sinseoldong	신설동	新设洞	②	0.9	44.8
●	●	127	Dongmyo	동묘앞	东庙	⑥	0.7	45.5
●	●	128	Dongdaemun	동대문	东大门	④	0.6	46.1
	●	129	Jongno 5(o)-ga	종로5가	钟路五街		0.8	46.9
●	●	130	Jongno 3(sam)-ga	종로3가	钟路三街	③ ⑤	0.9	47.8

		#	ENG	KOR	CHN	TRANSFER	DISTANCE (km)	ACCUM. DISTANCE (km)
	●	131	Jonggak	종각	钟阁		0.8	48.6
●	●	132	City Hall	시청	市厅	2	1	49.6
	●	133	Seoul Station	서울역	首尔(站)	4	1.1	50.7
●		134	Namyeong	남영	南营		1.7	52.4
●		135	Yongsan	용산	龙山		1.5	53.9
		136	Noryangjin	노량진	鹭梁津	9	2.6	56.5
●		137	Daebang	대방	大方		1.5	58
●		138	Singil	신길	新吉	5	0.8	58.8
		139	Yeongdeungpo	영등포	永登浦		1	59.8
●		140	Sindorim	신도림	新道林	2	1.5	61.3
●		141	Guro	구로	九老	1 *	1.1	62.4
●		142	Guil	구일	九一		1.4	63.8
		143	Gaebong	개봉	开峰		1	64.8
		144	Oryu-dong	오류동	梧柳洞		1.3	66.1
		145	Onsu	온수	温水	7	1.9	68
		146	Yeokgok	역곡	驿谷		1.3	69.3
		147	Sosa	소사	素砂		1.5	70.8
		148	Bucheon	부천	富川		1.1	71.9
		149	Jung-dong	중동	中洞		1.7	73.6
		150	Songnae	송내	松内		1	74.6
		151	Bugae	부개	富开		1.2	75.8
●		152	Bupyeong	부평	富平		1.5	77.3
		153	Baegun	백운	白云		1.7	79
		154	Dongam	동암	铜岩		1.5	80.5
●		155	Ganseok	간석	间石		1.2	81.7
●		156	Juan	주안	朱安		1.2	82.9
		157	Dohwa	도화	道禾		1	83.9
		158	Jemulpo	제물포	济物浦		1	84.9
		159	Dowon	도원	桃源		1.4	86.3
		160	Dongincheon	동인천	东仁川		1.2	87.5
		161	Incheon	인천	仁川		1.9	89.4

141 Guro splits to a separate branch (south bound), which is denoted with a P in front. Continued on the next page.

👫	🔒	#	ENG	KOR	CHN	TRANSFER	DISTANCE (km)	ACCUM. DISTANCE (km)
		P142	Gasan Digital Complex	가산디지털단지	加山数码园区	⑦	2.4	64.8
		P143	Doksan	독산	禿山		2	66.8
		P144	Geumcheon-gu Office	금천구청	衿川区厅	①*	1.2	68
		P144-1	Gwangmyeong	광명	光明	①*.KTX	4.7	N/A
●		P145	Seoksu	석수	石水		2.3	70.3
●		P146	Gwanak	관악	冠岳		1.9	72.2
		P147	Anyang	안양	安养		2.4	74.6
●		P148	Myeonghak	명학	鸣鹤		2.2	76.8
●		P149	Geumjeong	금정	衿井	④	1.4	78.2
		P150	Gunpo	군포	军浦		2.2	80.4
		P151	Dangjeong	당정	堂井		1.6	82
		P152	Uiwang	의왕	义王		2.6	84.6
●		P153	Sungkyunkwan Univ.	성균관대	成均馆大学		2.9	87.5
●		P154	Hwaseo	화서	华西		2.6	90.1
●		P155	Suwon	수원	水原		2.1	92.2
		P156	Seryu	세류	细柳		2.9	95.1
		P157	Byeongjeom	병점	饼店	①*	4.3	99.4
		P157-1	Seodongtan	서동탄	西东滩	①*	2.2	N/A
		P158	Sema	세마	西东滩		2.4	101.8
		P159	Osan Univ.	오산대	洗马		2.7	104.5
		P160	Osan	오산	乌山大学		2.7	107.2
		P161	Jinwi	진위	乌山		4	111.2
		P162	Songtan	송탄	振威		3.8	115
		P163	Seojeongni	서정리	松炭		2.2	117.2
		P164	Pyeongtaekjije	평택지제	西井里		4.8	122
		P165	Pyeongtaek	평택	芝制		3.7	125.7
		P166	Seonghwan	성환	平泽		9.4	135.1
		P167	Jiksan	직산	成欢		5.4	140.5
		P168	Dujeong	두정	稷山		3.8	144.3
		P169	Cheonan	천안	斗井		3	147.3
		P170	Bongmyeong	봉명	天安		1.5	148.8
		P171	Ssangyong (Korea Nazarene Univ.)	쌍용(나사렛대)	凤鸣		1.5	150.3
		P172	Asan	아산	双龙(拿撒勒大学)		1.5	151.8
		P173	Tangjeong	탕정	牙山		1.8	153.6
		P174	Baebang	배방	排芳		3.1	156.7
		P176	Onyangoncheon	온양온천	温阳温泉		4.9	161.6
		P177	Sinchang (Soonchunhyang Univ.)	신창(순천향대)	新昌		5.1	166.7

P144 Geumcheon-gu Office connects to P144-1 Gwangmyeong, which is the only stop of the branch.

P157 Byeongjeom connects to P157-1 Seodongtan, which is the only stop of the branch. Distance between the two is 4.7km.

👪	🔒	#	ENG	KOR	CHN	TRANSFER	DISTANCE (km)	ACCUM. DISTANCE (km)
●	●	201	City Hall	시청	市厅	❶		
	●	202	Euljiro 1(il)-ga	을지로입구	乙支路入口		0.7	0.7
●	●	203	Euljiro 3(sam)-ga	을지로3가	乙支路三街	❸	0.8	1.5
	●	204	Euljiro 4(sa)-ga	을지로4가	乙支路四街	❺	0.6	2.1
●	●	205	Dongdaemun History & Culture Park	동대문역사문화공원	东大门历史文化公园	❹ ❺	1	3.1
	●	206	Sindang	신당	新堂	❻	0.9	4
	●	207	Sangwangsimni	상왕십리	上往十里		0.9	4.9
●	●	208	Wangsimni	왕십리	往十里	❺	0.8	5.7
	●	209	Hanyang Univ.	한양대	汉阳大学		1	6.7
	●	210	Ttukseom	뚝섬	纛岛		1.1	7.8
	●	211	Seongsu	성수	圣水	❷ -1*	0.8	8.6
●	●	212	Konkuk Univ.	건대입구	建国大学	❼	1.2	9.8
	●	213	Guui(Gwangjin-gu Office)	구의(광진구청)	九宜		1.6	11.4
	●	214	Gangbyeon(Dongseoul Bus Terminal)	강변(동서울터미널)	江边(东首尔客运站)		0.9	12.3
	●	215	Jamsillaru	잠실나루	蚕室渡口		1.8	14.1
	●	216	Jamsil(Songpa-gu Office)	잠실(송파구청)	蚕室(松坡区厅)	❽	1	15.1
	●	217	Jamsilsaenae	잠실새내	蚕室新川		1.2	16.3
●	●	218	Sports Complex	종합운동장	综合运动场	❾	1.2	17.5
	●	219	Samseong(World Trade Center Seoul)	삼성(무역센터)	三成(会展中心)		1	18.5
	●	220	Seolleung	선릉	宣陵		1.3	19.8
	●	221	Yeoksam	역삼	驿三		1.2	21
●	●	222	Gangnam	강남	江南		0.8	21.8
	●	223	"Seoul Nat'l Univ. of Education (Court & Public Prosecutors' Office)"	교대(법원·검찰청)	首尔教育大学	❸	1.2	23
	●	224	Seocho	서초	瑞草		0.7	23.7
	●	225	Bangbae(Baekseok Arts Univ.)	방배(백석예술대)	方背		1.7	25.4
	●	226	Sadang	사당	舍堂	❹	1.6	27
	●	227	Nakseongdae	낙성대	落星垈		1.7	28.7
	●	228	Seoul Nat'l Univ.(Gwanak-gu Office)	서울대입구 (관악구청)	首尔大学(冠岳区厅)		1	29.7
	●	229	Bongcheon	봉천	奉天		1	30.7
	●	230	Sillim	신림	新林		1.1	31.8
●	●	231	Sindaebang	신대방	新大方		1.8	33.6
●	●	232	Guro Digital Complex (Wonkwang Digital Univ.)	구로디지털단지 (원광디지털대)	九老数码园区		1.1	34.7

👥	🔒	#	ENG	KOR	CHN	TRANSFER	DISTANCE (km)	ACCUM. DISTANCE (km)
●	●	233	Daerim(Guro-gu Office)	대림(구로구청)	大林	7	1.1	35.8
●	●	234	Sindorim	신도림	新道林	1 2 -2*	1.8	37.6
	●	235	Mullae	문래	文来		1.2	38.8
●	●	236	Yeongdeungpo-gu Office	영등포구청	永登浦区厅	5	0.9	39.7
●	●	237	Dangsan	당산	堂山	9	1.1	40.8
	●	238	Hapjeong	합정	合井	6	2	42.8
	●	239	Hongik Univ.	홍대입구	弘益大学		1.1	43.9
	●	240	Sinchon	신촌	新村		1.3	45.2
	●	241	Ewha Womans Univ.	이대	梨花女子大学		0.8	46
	●	242	Ahyeon(Chugye Univ. for the Arts)	아현(추계예술대)	阿岘		0.9	46.9
	●	243	Chungjeongno(Kyonggi Univ.)	충정로(경기대입구)	忠正路	5	0.8	47.7

2-1 Seongsu Branch

👥	🔒	#	ENG	KOR	CHN	TRANSFER	DISTANCE (km)	ACCUM. DISTANCE (km)
	●	211-1	Yongdap	용답	龙踏		2.3	2.3
●	●	211-2	Sindap	신답	新踏		1.0	3.3
●	●	211-3	Yongdu(Dongdaemun-gu Office)	용두(동대문구청)	龙头(东大门区厅)		0.9	4.2
●	●	211-4	Sinseoldong	신설동	新设洞	1	1.2	5.4

2-2 Sinjeong Branch

👥	🔒	#	ENG	KOR	CHN	TRANSFER	DISTANCE (km)	ACCUM. DISTANCE (km)
	●	234-1	Dorimcheon	도림천	道林川		1.0	1.0
●	●	234-2	Yangcheon-gu Office	양천구청	阳川区厅		1.7	2.7
	●	234-3	Sinjeongnegeori	신정네거리	新亭十字路口		1.9	4.6
		234-4	Kkachisan	까치산	喜鹊山	5	1.4	6.0

👪	🔒	#	ENG	KOR	CHN	TRANSFER	DISTANCE (km)	ACCUM. DISTANCE (km)
		309	Daehwa	대화	大化			
		310	Juyeop	주엽	注叶		1.4	1.4
		311	Jeongbalsan	정발산	鼎鉢山		1.6	3
		312	Madu	마두	马头		0.9	3.9
		313	Baekseok	백석	白石		1.4	5.3
●		314	Daegok	대곡	大谷		2.5	7.8
		315	Hwajeong	화정	花井		2.1	9.9
		316	Wondang	원당	元堂		2.6	12.5
		317	Wonheung	원흥	元兴		2.9	15.4
		318	Samsong	삼송	三松		2.1	17.5
●	●	319	Jichuk	지축	紙杻		1.7	19.2
	●	320	Gupabal	구파발	旧把拨		1.5	20.7
●	●	321	Yeonsinnae	연신내	延新川	⑥	2	22.7
	●	322	Bulgwang	불광	佛光	⑥	1.3	24
	●	323	Nokbeon	녹번	碌磻		1.1	25.1
	●	324	Hongje (Seoul Culture Arts Univ.)	홍제	弘济		1.6	26.7
●	●	325	Muakjae	무악재	毋岳岭		0.9	27.6
●	●	326	Dongnimmun	독립문	独立门		1.1	28.7
●	●	327	Gyeongbokgung (Government Complex-Seoul)	경복궁 (정부서울청사)	景福宫		1.6	30.3
	●	328	Anguk	안국	安国		1.1	31.4
●	●	329	Jongno 3(sam)-ga	종로3가	钟路三街	①⑤	1	32.4
●	●	330	Euljiro 3(sam)-ga (Shinhan Card)	을지로3가 (신한카드)	乙支路三街	②	0.6	33
●	●	331	Chungmuro	충무로	忠武路	④	0.7	33.7
●	●	332	Dongguk Univ.	동대입구	东国大学		0.9	34.6
●	●	333	Yaksu	약수	药水		0.7	35.3
●	●	334	Geumho	금호	金湖	⑥	0.8	36.1
	●	335	Oksu	옥수	玉水		0.8	36.9
	●	336	Apgujeong (Hyundai Department Store)	압구정(현대백화점)	狎鸥亭		2.1	39
	●	337	Sinsa	신사	新沙		1.5	40.5
●	●	338	Jamwon	잠원	蚕院	⑦⑨	0.9	41.4
	●	339	Express Bus Terminal	고속터미널	高速巴士客运站		1.2	42.6

♿	🔒	#	ENG	KOR	CHN	TRANSFER	DISTANCE (km)	ACCUM. DISTANCE (km)
	●	340	Seoul Nat'l Univ. of Education (Court & Public Prosecutor's Office)	교대(법원·검찰청)	首尔教育大学	②	1.6	44.2
●	●	341	Nambu Bus Terminal (Seoul Arts Center)	남부터미널 (예술의전당)	南部客运站		0.9	45.1
●	●	342	Yangjae(Seocho-gu Office)	양재(서초구청)	良才		1.8	46.9
	●	343	Maebong	매봉	梅峰		1.2	48.1
	●	344	Dogok	도곡	道谷		0.8	48.9
●	●	345	Daechi	대치	大峙		0.8	49.7
	●	346	Hangnyeoul	학여울	鹤滩		0.8	50.5
●	●	347	Daecheong	대청	大厅		0.9	51.4
	●	348	Irwon	일원	逸院		1.2	52.6
●	●	349	Suseo	수서	水西		1.8	54.4
●	●	350	Garak Market	가락시장	可乐市场	⑧	1.4	55.8
●	●	351	Nat'l Police Hospital	경찰병원	警察医院		0.8	56.6
●	●	352	Ogeum	오금	梧琴	⑤	0.8	57.4

👫	🔒	#	ENG	KOR	CHN	TRANSFER	DISTANCE (km)	ACCUM. DISTANCE (km)
	●	409	Danggogae	당고개	堂岭			
●	●	410	Sanggye	상계	上溪		1.2	1.2
●	●	411	Nowon	노원	芦原	⑦	1	2.2
●	●	412	Chang-dong	창동	仓洞	①	1.4	3.6
●	●	413	Ssangmun	쌍문	双门		1.3	4.9
●	●	414	Suyu (Gangbuk-gu Office)	수유(강북구청)	水逾		1.5	6.4
●	●	415	Mia (Seoul Cyber University)	미아(서울사이버대학)	彌阿		1.4	7.8
●	●	416	Miasageori	미아사거리	弥阿十字路口		1.5	9.3
●	●	417	Gireum	길음	吉音		1.3	10.6
●	●	418	Sungshin Women's University (Donam)	성신여대입구(돈암)	诚信女子大学(敦岩)		1.4	12
●	●	419	Hansung University (Samseongyo)	한성대입구(삼선교)	汉城大学(三仙桥)		1	13
●	●	420	Hyehwa	혜화	惠化		0.9	13.9
●	●	421	Dongdaemun	동대문	东大门	①	1.5	15.4
●	●	422	Dongdaemun History & Culture Park (DDP)	동대문역사문화공원(DDP)	东大门历史文化公园	② ⑤	0.7	16.1
●	●	423	Chungmuro	충무로	忠武路	③	1.3	17.4
●	●	424	Myeong-dong	명동(정화예술대)	明洞		0.7	18.1
●	●	425	Hoehyeon (Namdaemun Market)	회현(남대문시장)	会贤(南大门市场)		0.7	18.8
	●	426	Seoul Station	서울역	首尔(站)	①	0.9	19.7
	●	427	Sookmyung Women's University (Garwol)	숙대입구(갈월)	淑明女子大学(葛月)		1	20.7
●	●	428	Samgakji	삼각지	三角地	⑥	1.2	21.9
	●	429	Sinyongsan (AMOREPACIFIC)	신용산(아모레퍼시픽)	新龙山		0.7	22.6
●	●	430	Ichon (National Museum of Korea)	이촌(국립중앙박물관)	二村		1.3	23.9
●	●	431	Dongjak (Seoul National Cemetery)	동작(현충원)	铜雀	⑨	2.7	26.6
●	●	432	Chongsin University (Isu)	총신대입구(이수)	总神大学(梨水)	⑦	1.8	28.4
●	●	433	Sadang	사당	舍堂	②	1.1	29.5
●	●	434	Namtaeryeong	남태령	南泰岭		1.6	31.1
		435	Seonbawi	선바위	立岩		2	33.1
		436	Seoul Racecourse Park	경마공원	竞马公园		1	34.1
		437	Seoul Grand Park	대공원 (서울랜드)	首尔大公园		0.9	35
●		438	Gwacheon	과천	果川		1	36
●		439	Government Complex Gwacheon	정부과천청사	政府果川厅舍		1	37
		440	Indeogwon	인덕원	仁德院		3	40
		441	Pyeongchon	평촌	坪村		1.6	41.6
		442	Beomgye	범계	凡溪		1.3	42.9

👥	🔒	#	ENG	KOR	CHN	TRANSFER	DISTANCE (km)	ACCUM. DISTANCE (km)
●		443	Geumjeong	금정	衿井	①	2.6	45.5
		444	Sanbon	산본	山本		2.3	47.8
		445	Surisan	수리산	修理山		1.1	48.9
		446	Daeyami	대야미	大夜味		2.6	51.5
		447	Banwol	반월	半月		2	53.5
●		448	Sangnoksu	상록수	常绿树		3.7	57.2
●		449	Hanyang University at Ansan	한대앞	汉阳大学(安山)		1.5	58.7
●		450	Jungang	중앙	中央		1.6	60.3
●		451	Gojan	고잔	古栈		1.4	61.7
●		452	Choji	초지	草芝		1.5	63.2
		453	Ansan	안산	安山		1.8	65
		454	Singiloncheon	신길온천	新吉溫泉		2.2	67.2
		455	Jeongwang	정왕	正往		2.9	70.1
		456	Oido	오이도	烏耳島		1.4	71.5

👫	🔒	#	ENG	KOR	CHN	TRANSFER	DISTANCE (km)	ACCUM. DISTANCE (km)
	●	510	Banghwa	방화	傍花			
	●	511	Gaehwasan	개화산	开花山		0.9	0.9
	●	512	Gimpo Int'l Airport	김포공항	金浦机场	9	1.2	2.1
	●	513	Songjeong	송정	松亭		1.2	3.3
	●	514	Magok(Home & Shopping)	마곡(홈앤쇼핑)	麻谷		1.1	4.4
	●	515	Balsan	발산	钵山		1.2	5.6
	●	516	Ujangsan	우장산	雨装山		1.1	6.7
	●	517	Hwagok	화곡	禾谷		1	7.7
	●	518	Kkachisan	까치산	喜鹊山	2	1.2	8.9
●	●	519	Sinjeong(Eunhaengjeong)	신정(은행정)	新亭		1.3	10.2
	●	520	Mok-dong	목동	木洞		0.8	11
	●	521	Omokgyo (Mokdong Stadium)	오목교(목동운동장앞)	梧木桥(木洞运动场)		0.9	11.9
●	●	522	Yangpyeong	양평	杨坪		1.1	13
	●	523	Yeongdeungpo-gu Office	영등포구청	永登浦区厅	2	0.8	13.8
	●	524	Yeongdeungpo Market (Hallym Univ. Hanggang Sacred Heart Hospital)	영등포시장 (한림대 한강성심병원)	永登浦市场		0.9	14.7
	●	525	Singil	신길	新吉	1	1.1	15.8
●	●	526	Yeouido	여의도	汝矣岛	9	1	16.8
	●	527	Yeouinaru	여의나루	汝矣渡口		1	17.8
	●	528	Mapo	마포	麻浦		1.8	19.6
		529	Gongdeok	공덕	孔德	6	0.8	20.4
	●	530	Aeogae	애오개	儿岭		1.1	21.5
	●	531	Chungjeongno(Kyonggi Univ.)	충정로(경기대입구)	忠正路	2	0.9	22.4
	●	532	Seodaemun(Kangbuk Samsung Hospital)	서대문(강북삼성병원)	西大门		0.7	23.1
	●	533	Gwanghwamun (Sejong Center for the Perfoming Arts)	광화문(세종문화회관)	光化门(世宗文化会馆)		1.1	24.2
●	●	534	Jongno 3(sam)-ga(Tapgol Park)	종로3가(탑골공원)	钟路三街	1 3	1.2	25.4
	●	535	Euljiro 4(sa)-ga	을지로4가	乙支路四街	2	1	26.4
	●	536	Dongdaemun History & Culture Park	동대문역사문화공원(DDP)	东大门历史文化公园	2 4	0.9	27.3
	●	537	Cheonggu	청구	青丘	6	0.9	28.2
	●	538	Singeumho	신금호	新金湖		0.9	29.1
	●	539	Haengdang	행당	杏堂		0.8	29.9
●	●	540	Wangsimni(SeongDong-Gu Office)	왕십리(성동구청)	往十里	2	0.9	30.8

👥	🔒	#	ENG	KOR	CHN	TRANSFER	DISTANCE (km)	ACCUM. DISTANCE (km)
	●	541	Majang	마장	马场		0.7	31.5
	●	542	Dapsimni	답십리	踏十里		1	32.5
	●	543	Janghanpyeong	장한평	长汉坪		1.2	33.7
	●	544	Gunja(Neung-dong)	군자(능동)	君子(陵洞)	⑦	1.5	35.2
	●	545	Achasan (Rear Entrance to Seoul Children's Grand Park)	아차산 (어린이대공원후문)	峨嵯山		1	36.2
	●	546	Gangnaru (Presbyterian Univ. & College & Seminary)	광나루(장신대)	广渡口(长神大学)		1.5	37.7
	●	547	Cheonho (Pungnaptoseong)	천호(풍납토성)	千戶	⑧	2	39.7
	●	548	Gangdong	강동	江东	⑤ -1	0.8	40.5
	●	549	Gil-dong	길동	吉洞		0.9	41.4
	●	550	Gubeundari (Gangdong Community Center)	굽은다리(강동구민회관앞)	曲桥(江东区民会馆)		0.8	42.2
	●	551	Myeongil	명일	明逸		0.7	42.9
	●	552	Godeok(Kyung Hee Univ. Hospital at Gangdong)	고덕(강동경희대병원)	高德		1.2	44.1
	●	553	Sangil-dong	상일동	上一洞		1.1	45.2

5-1 Macheon Branch

👥	🔒	#	ENG	KOR	CHN	TRANSFER	DISTANCE (km)	ACCUM. DISTANCE (km)
	●	P549	Dunchon-dong	둔촌동	遁村洞		1.2	1.2
●	●	P550	Olympic Park (Korean National Sport Univ.)	올림픽공원(한국체대)	奥林匹克公园 (韩国体育大学)	⑨	1.4	2.6
	●	P551	Bangi	방이	芳荑		0.9	3.5
●	●	P552	Ogeum	오금	梧琴	③	0.9	4.4
	●	P553	Gaerong	개롱	开笼		0.9	5.3
	●	P554	Geoyeo	거여	巨余		0.9	6.2
	●	P555	Macheon	마천	马川		0.9	7.1

♿	🔒	#	ENG	KOR	CHN	TRANSFER	DISTANCE (km)	ACCUM. DISTANCE (km)
	●	610	Eungam	응암	鷹岩			
	●	611	Yeokchon	역촌	驿村		1.1	1.1
	●	612	Bulgwang	불광	佛光	3	0.8	1.9
	●	613	Dokbawi	독바위	瓮岩		0.9	2.8
	●	614	Yeonsinnae	연신내	延新川	3	1.4	4.2
	●	615	Gusan	구산	龟山		0.9	5.1
	●	616	Saejeol(Sinsa)	새절(신사)	赛折(新寺)		0.9	6
	●	617	Jeungsan(Myongji Univ.)	증산(명지대앞)	缯山(明知大学)		0.9	6.9
●	●	618	Digital Media City	디지털미디어시티	数码媒体城		1.1	8
●	●	619	World Cup Stadium(Seongsan)	월드컵경기장(성산)	世界杯体育场		0.8	8.8
	●	620	Mapo-gu Office	마포구청	麻浦区厅		0.8	9.6
	●	621	Mangwon	망원	望远		1	10.6
	●	622	Hapjeong	합정	合井	2	0.8	11.4
	●	623	Sangsu	상수	上水		0.8	12.2
	●	622	Hapjeong	합정	合井	2	0.8	11.4
	●	623	Sangsu	상수	上水		0.8	12.2
	●	624	Gwangheungchang(Seogang)	광흥창(서강)	广兴仓		0.9	13.1
	●	625	Daeheung(Sogang Univ.)	대흥(서강대앞)	大兴(西江大学)		1	14.1
	●	626	Gongdeok	공덕	孔德	5	0.9	15
	●	627	Hyochang Park	효창공원앞	孝昌公园		0.9	15.9
	●	628	Samgakji	삼각지	三角地	4	1.2	17.1
	●	629	Noksapyeong(Yongsan-gu Office)	녹사평(용산구청앞)	绿莎坪		1.1	18.2
	●	630	Itaewon	이태원	梨泰院		0.8	19
●	●	631	Hangangjin	한강진	汉江镇		1	20
	●	632	Beotigogae	버티고개	波提岭		1	21
●	●	633	Yaksu	약수	药水	3	0.7	21.7
		634	Cheonggu	청구	青丘	5	0.8	22.5
	●	635	Sindang	신당	新堂	2	0.7	23.2
	●	636	Dongmyo	동묘앞	东庙	1	0.6	23.8
●	●	637	Changsin	창신	昌信		0.9	24.7
	●	638	Bomun	보문	普门		0.8	25.5
●	●	639	Anam(Korea Univ. Hospital)	안암(고대병원앞)	安岩		0.9	26.4
●	●	640	Korea Univ.(Jongam)	고려대(종암)	高丽大学(钟岩)		0.8	27.2
	●	641	Wolgok(Dongduk Women's Univ.)	월곡(동덕여대)	月谷		1.4	28.6
	●	642	Sangwolgok(KIST)	상월곡(한국과학기술연구원)	上月谷		0.8	29.4
	●	643	Dolgoji	돌곶이	石串		0.8	30.2

👫	🔒	#	ENG	KOR	CHN	TRANSFER	DISTANCE (km)	ACCUM. DISTANCE (km)
●	●	644	Seokgye	석계	石溪	❶	1	31.2
		645	Taereung	태릉입구	泰陵	❼	0.8	32
	●	646	Hwarangdae(Seoul Women's Univ.)	화랑대(서울여대입구)	花郎台 (首尔女子大学)		0.9	32.9
	●	647	Bonghwasan(Seoul Medical Center)	봉화산(서울의료원)	烽火山		0.7	33.6
		648	Sinnae	신내	新內		1.3	34.9

		#	ENG	KOR	CHN	TRANSFER	DISTANCE (km)	ACCUM. DISTANCE (km)
		709	Jangam	장암	长岩	❶		
●	●	710	Dobongsan	도봉산	道峰山		1.4	1.4
	●	711	Suraksan	수락산	水落山		1.6	3
	●	712	Madeul	마들	马得		1.4	4.4
	●	713	Nowon	노원	芦原	④	1.2	5.6
	●	714	Junggye(Korean Bible Univ.)	중계(한국성서대)	中溪		1.1	6.7
	●	715	Hagye(Eulji Medical Center)	하계(을지대 을지병원)	下溪		1	7.7
	●	716	Gongneung (Seoul Nat'l Univ. of Science and Technology)	공릉(서울과학기술대)	孔陵		1.3	9
	●	717	Taereung	태릉입구	泰陵	❻	0.8	9.8
	●	718	Meokgol	먹골	墨谷		0.9	10.7
	●	719	Junghwa	중화	中和		0.9	11.6
●	●	720	Sangbong(Intercity Bus Terminal)	상봉(시외버스터미널)	上凤 (市外巴士客运站)		1	12.6
	●	721	Myeonmok	면목	面牧		0.8	13.4
	●	722	Sagajeong(Green Hospital)	사가정(녹색병원)	四佳亭		0.9	14.3
	●	723	Yongmasan(Yongma Falls Park)	용마산(용마폭포공원)	四佳亭		0.8	15.1
	●	724	Junggok	중곡	中谷		0.9	16
		725	Gunja(Neung-dong)	군자(능동)	君子(陵洞)	❺	1.1	17.1
	●	726	Children's Grand Park(Sejong Univ.)	어린이대공원(세종대)	儿童大公园 (世宗大学)		1.1	18.2
●	●	727	Konkuk University	건대입구	建国大学	②	0.8	19
●	●	728	Ttukseom Park	뚝섬유원지	纛岛游园地		1	20
	●	729	Cheongdam(Korea Gold Exchange)	청담(한국금거래소)	清潭		2	22
	●	730	Gangnam-gu Office	강남구청	江南区厅		1.1	23.1
	●	731	Hak-dong	학동	鹤洞		0.9	24
	●	732	Nonhyeon	논현	论岘		1	25
	●	733	Banpo	반포	盘浦		0.9	25.9
	●	734	Express Bus Terminal	고속터미널	高速巴士客运站	❸ ❾	0.9	26.8
	●	735	Naebang	내방	內方		2.2	29
●	●	736	Isu(Chongsin University)	이수(총신대입구)	梨水	④	1	30
●	●	737	Namseong	남성	南城		1	31
	●	738	Soongsil Univ.(Salpijae)	숭실대입구(살피재)	崇实大学(赛毗陵)		2	33
	●	739	Sangdo	상도	上道		0.9	33.9
	●	740	Jangseungbaegi	장승배기	长丞拜基		0.9	34.8
	●	741	Sindaebangsamgeori	신대방삼거리	新大方丁字路口		1.2	36
	●	742	Boramae	보라매	波拉美		0.8	36.8

👥	🔒	#	ENG	KOR	CHN	TRANSFER	DISTANCE (km)	ACCUM. DISTANCE (km)
	●	743	Sinpung	신풍	新丰		0.9	37.7
●	●	744	Daerim(Guro-gu Office)	대림(구로구청)	大林	2	1.4	39.1
	●	745	Namguro	남구로	南九老		1.1	40.2
	●	746	Gasan Digital Complex(Mario Outlet)	가산디지털단지 (마리오아울렛)	加山数码园区	1	0.8	41
	●	747	Cheolsan	철산	铁山		1.4	42.4
	●	748	Gwangmyeongsageori	광명사거리	光明十字路口		1.3	43.7
	●	749	Cheonwang	천왕	天旺		1.7	45.4
	●	750	Onsu(Sungkonghoe Univ.)	온수(성공회대입구)	温水(圣公会大学)		1.5	46.9
		751	Kkachiul	까치울	喜鹊屋		2.2	49.1
●		752	Bucheon Stadium	부천종합운동장	富川綜合運動場		1.2	50.3
		753	Chunui	춘의	春衣		0.9	51.2
		754	Sinjung-dong	신중동	新中洞		1	52.2
		755	Bucheon City Hall	부천시청	富川市厅		1.1	53.3
		756	Sang-dong	상동	上洞		0.9	54.2
		757	Samsan Gymnasium	삼산체육관	三山体育馆		1.1	55.3
		758	Gulpocheon	굴포천	掘浦川		0.9	56.2
●		759	Bupyeong-gu Office	부평구청	富平区厅		0.9	57.1
		760	Sangok	산곡	儿童大公园 (世宗大学)		1.6	58.7
●		761	Seoknam(Geobuk Market)	석남(거북시장)	建国大学		2.3	61

		#	ENG	KOR	CHN	TRANSFER	DISTANCE (km)	ACCUM. DISTANCE (km)
	●	810	Amsa	암사	岩寺			
		811	Cheonho(Pungnaptoseong)	천호(풍납토성)	千户(风纳土城)	5	1.3	1.3
	●	812	Gangdong-gu Office	강동구청	江东区厅		0.9	2.2
	●	813	Mongchontoseong(World Peace Gate)	몽촌토성(평화의문)	梦村土城(平和之门)		1.6	3.8
	●	814	Jamsil(Songpa-gu Office)	잠실(송파구청)	蚕室(松坡区厅)	2	0.8	4.6
●	●	815	Seokchon(Hansol Hospital)	석촌(한솔병원)	石村	9	1.2	5.8
	●	816	Songpa	송파	松坡		0.9	6.7
●	●	817	Garak Market	가락시장	可乐市场	3	0.8	7.5
	●	818	Munjeong	문정	文井		0.9	8.4
	●	819	Jangji	장지	长旨		0.9	9.3
	●	820	Bokjeong	복정	福井		0.9	10.2
	●	821	Namwirye	남위례	南慰礼		1.6	11.8
	●	822	Sanseong	산성	山城		1.1	12.9
	●	823	Namhansanseong(Seongnam Court & Prosecutor's Office)	남한산성입구 (성남법원·검찰청)	南汉山城 (城南法院·检察厅)		1.3	14.2
	●	824	Dandaeogeori(Shingu College)	단대오거리 (신구대학교)	丹垈五岔路口		0.8	15.0
	●	825	Sinheung	신흥	新兴		0.8	15.8
	●	826	Sujin	수진	寿进		0.9	16.7
	●	827	Moran	모란	牡丹		1.0	17.7

🚻	🔒	#	ENG	KOR	CHN	TRANSFER	DISTANCE (km)	ACCUM. DISTANCE (km)
	●	901	Gaehwa	개화	开花			
●	●	902	Gimpo Int'l Airport	김포공항	金浦机场	5	3.6	3.6
		903	Airport Market	공항시장	机场市场		0.8	4.4
	●	904	Sinbanghwa	신방화	新傍花		0.8	5.2
		905	Magongnaru	마곡나루(서울식물원)	麻谷渡口		0.9	6.1
	●	906	Yangcheon Hyanggyo	양천향교	阳川乡校		1.4	7.5
	●	907	Gayang	가양	加阳		1.3	8.8
	●	908	Jeungmi	증미	曾米		0.7	9.5
	●	909	Deungchon	등촌	登村		1.0	10.5
	●	910	Yeomchang	염창	盐仓		0.9	11.4
	●	911	Sinmokdong	신목동	新木洞		0.9	12.3
	●	912	Seonyudo	선유도	仙游岛		1.2	13.5
●	●	913	Dangsan	당산	堂山	2	1.0	14.5
●	●	914	National Assembly	국회의사당 (KDB산업은행)	国会议事堂		1.5	16.0
●	●	915	Yeouido	여의도	汝矣岛	5	0.9	16.9
	●	916	Saetgang	샛강(KB금융타운)	赛江		0.8	17.7
●	●	917	Noryangjin	노량진	鹭梁津	1	1.2	18.9
	●	918	Nodeul	노들	鹭得		1.1	20.0
	●	919	Heukseok (Chung-Ang Univ.)	흑석(중앙대입구)	黑石(中央大学)		1.1	21.1
●	●	920	Dongjak (Seoul National Cemetery)	동작(현충원)	铜雀(显忠院)	4	1.4	22.5
	●	921	Gubanpo	구반포	旧盘浦		1.0	23.5
	●	922	Sinbanpo	신반포	新盘浦		0.7	24.2
●	●	923	Express Bus Terminal	고속터미널	高速巴士客运站	3 7	0.8	25.0
		924	Sapyeong	사평	砂平		1.1	26.1
	●	925	Sinnonhyeon (Le Meridien Hotel)	신논현(르메르디앙호텔)	新论岘		0.9	27.0
	●	926	Eonju (CHA Gangnam Medical Center)	연주(강남차병원)	彦州		0.8	27.8
	●	927	Seonjeongneung	선정릉	宣靖陵		0.9	28.7
	●	928	Samseongjungang	삼성중앙	三成中央		0.8	29.5
	●	929	Bongeunsa	봉은사	奉恩寺		0.8	30.3
●	●	930	Sports Complex	종합운동장	综合运动场	2	1.4	31.7
		931	Samjeon	삼전	三田		1.4	33.1
		932	Seokchon Gobun	석촌고분	石村古坟		0.8	33.9
●		933	Seokchon	석촌	石村	8	1.0	34.9
		934	Songpanaru	송파나루	松坡渡口		0.8	35.7
		935	Hanseong Baekje	한성백제	汉城百济		0.8	36.5
●		936	Olympic Park	올림픽공원(한국체대)	奥林匹克公园	5	1.4	37.9
		937	Dunchon Oryun	둔촌오륜	遁村五轮		1.0	38.9
		938	VHS Medical Center	중앙보훈병원	中央报勋医院		1.7	40.6

REFERENCES & CREDITS

| Amore Pacific Museum of Art | 안리나나, CC BY 2.0 KR <https://creativecommons.org/licenses/by/2.0/kr/> via https://blog.naver.com/alli_nana/222743599389 |

Apgujeong Rodeo Street — 초묵초묵 어흥이, CC BY 2.0 KR <https://creativecommons.org/licenses/by/2.0/kr/> via https://blog.naver.com/day265/222652157391

Amsa-dong Prehistoric Settlement Site — G4Jm8, CC BY-SA 4.0 <https://creativecommons.org/licenses/by-sa/4.0>, via Wikimedia Commons

Boramae Park — Im9128, CC BY 2.0 KR <https://creativecommons.org/licenses/by/2.0/kr/> via https://blog.naver.com/im9128/222102649437

Central City — Pectus Solentis, CC BY-SA 2.0 <https://creativecommons.org/licenses/by-sa/2.0>, via Wikimedia Commons

COEX — lohasteru, CC BY-ND 2.0 <https://creativecommons.org/licenses/by-nd/2.0/> via https://www.flickr.com/photos/lohasteru/7079246065

Common Ground — Oooobit, CC BY-ND 2.0 KR <https://creativecommons.org/licenses/by-nd/2.0/kr/> via https://blog.naver.com/today930809/222720797538

Chungmu Art Center — 연, CC BY-ND 2.0 KR <https://creativecommons.org/licenses/by-nd/2.0/kr/> via https://blog.naver.com/ssovely8/222600567771

Dapsimni Antique Art Street — Jez Nicholson, CC BY-SA 2.0 <https://creativecommons.org/licenses/by-sa/2.0>, via https://www.flickr.com/photos/jnicho02/221566429

Dasan Digital Complex Outlet Town — 일상생략 및 방문후기, CC BY 2.0 KR <https://creativecommons.org/licenses/by/2.0/kr/> via https://blog.naver.com/smson97/220647329373

Goto Mall — 틱가이버, CC BY 2.0 KR <https://creativecommons.org/licenses/by/2.0/kr/> via https://blog.naver.com/tacgyber/222697288578

Haegeong Buckle Museum — Asfreeas, CC BY-SA 3.0 <https://creativecommons.org/licenses/by-sa/3.0>, via Wikimedia Commons

Heunginjimun Altar — RYU Cheol, CC BY-SA 3.0 <https://creativecommons.org/licenses/by-sa/3.0>, via Wikimedia Commons

IFC MALL — Seoul Guide Korea, CC BY 2.0 <https://creativecommons.org/licenses/by/2.0/> via https://www.flickr.com/photos/86137128@N07/8404989590

Incheon Chinatown — Riodaniscus, CC BY-SA 4.0 <https://creativecommons.org/licenses/by-sa/4.0>, via Wikimedia Commons

Itaewon Special Tourist Zone — Jay Yoo, CC BY-ND 2.0 <https://creativecommons.org/licenses/by-nd/2.0>, via https://www.flickr.com/photos/147789682@N06/33238618266

Jeoldusan Martyr's Shrine — Michael Gallagher, CC BY-SA 2.0 <https://creativecommons.org/licenses/by-sa/2.0>, via https://www.flickr.com/photos/michaelgallagher/14705216454

Jeong Dong Methodist Church — Ryuch, CC BY-SA 3.0 <https://creativecommons.org/licenses/by-sa/3.0>, via Wikimedia Commons

K Star Road — Matt Kieffer, CC BY-SA 2.0 <https://creativecommons.org/licenses/by-sa/2.0>, via https://www.flickr.com/photos/mattkieffer/48661242872

KINTEX — Min-Jung KIM, CC BY-SA 2.0 <https://creativecommons.org/licenses/by-sa/2.0>, via https://www.flickr.com/photos/129374898@N04/15874272839

Lotte World — Khitai (a flickr user), CC BY-SA 2.0 <https://creativecommons.org/licenses/by-sa/2.0>, via Wikimedia Commons

Map of Seoul — Wikipedia (benutzer:ralf roletschek) user [[:Benutzer:Ralf Roletschek:User {{{3}}}|{{{3}}}]], CC BY-SA 3.0 <http://creativecommons.org/licenses/by-sa/3.0/>, via Wikimedia Commons

Marronier Park — Scarlet Sappho, CC BY-SA 2.0 <https://creativecommons.org/licenses/by-sa/2.0>, via https://www.flickr.com/photos/skinnylawyer/5481260240

Mecenatpolis Mall — Travel Oriented, CC BY-SA 2.0 <https://creativecommons.org/licenses/by-sa/2.0>, via https://www.flickr.com/photos/traveloriented/11921840036

Nagwon Instrument Arcade — Republic of Korea, CC BY-SA 2.0 <https://creativecommons.org/licenses/by-sa/2.0>, via https://www.flickr.com/photos/koreanet/33235846020

National Chongdong Theater — 소담, CC BY 2.0 KR <https://creativecommons.org/licenses/by/2.0/kr/> via https://blog.naver.com/eao0926/222256714682

Olympic Park — Silas Low, CC BY-SA 4.0 <https://creativecommons.org/licenses/by-sa/4.0>, via Wikimedia Commons

Samcheongdong Cafe Road — Travel Oriented, CC BY-SA 2.0 <https://creativecommons.org/licenses/by-sa/2.0>, via https://www.flickr.com/photos/traveloriented/14938329291

Samjeondobi Stone Monument — Kang-Byeong Kee, CC BY 3.0 <https://creativecommons.org/licenses/by/3.0>, via Wikimedia Commons

Sejong Center — Marcopolis at en.wikipedia, Public domain, via Wikimedia Commons

Seorae Village & Montmartre Park — eao0926, CC BY-SA 2.0 KR <https://creativecommons.org/licenses/by-sa/2.0/kr/> via https://blog.naver.com/eao0926/222221109479

Seoul Folk Flea Market — Republic of Korea, CC BY-SA 2.0 <https://creativecommons.org/licenses/by-sa/2.0>, via https://www.flickr.com/photos/koreanet/8641373889

Seoul Museum of History — Jjw, CC BY-SA 3.0 <https://creativecommons.org/licenses/by-sa/3.0>, via Wikimedia Commons

Seoul National Cemetery — Kys951, Public domain, via Wikimedia Commons

Seoul Plaza — 서울시 총무과, CC BY-SA 4.0 <https://creativecommons.org/licenses/by-sa/4.0>, via Wikimedia Commons

Seoul World Cup Stadium — Photo and Share CC, CC BY 2.0 <https://creativecommons.org/licenses/by/2.0>, via Wikimedia Commons

Sinsadong Garosu-gil — 꿈꾸는여행 도도, CC BY 2.0 KR <https://creativecommons.org/licenses/by/2.0/kr/> via https://blog.naver.com/travelerdodo/222746451352

Subway Station — 뽀뽀니, CC BY 2.0 KR <https://creativecommons.org/licenses/by/2.0/kr/> via https://blog.naver.com/lovenget/221309142997

Tapgol Park — Steve46814, CC BY-SA 3.0 <https://creativecommons.org/licenses/by-sa/3.0>, via Wikimedia Commons

Times Square — Brit in Seoul, CC BY-SA 4.0 <https://creativecommons.org/licenses/by-sa/4.0>, via Wikimedia Commons

Yangcheon Hyanggyo Confucian School — 문화재청, KOGL Type 1 <http://www.kogl.or.kr/open/info/license_info/by.do>, via Wikimedia Commons

Youngnak Presbyterian Church — Davidabram at English Wikipedia, Public domain, via Wikimedia Commons

BEFORE VISITING KOREA

Consider the following titles for the best travel experience.

LET'S SPEAK KOREAN

Learn the essential Korean phrases to understand and interact with the Korean people. You will feel so much more welcomed.

KOREAN CULTURE DICTIONARY

Learn to understand Korean culture from A to Z! Get the most out of your trip by fully understanding all things Korean.

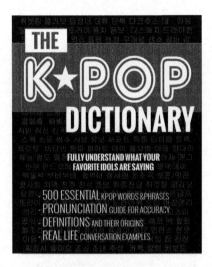

THE K-POP DICTIONARY

Learn the most popular words and phrases used in the K-pop scene so you can naturally spark a fun conversation with a Korean person, even if you are not a K-pop fan.

LET'S STUDY KOREAN

Complete Practice Work Book for Grammar, Spelling, Vocabulary and Reading Comprehension With Over 600 Questions.

KOREAN FOR EVERYONE

Complete Self-Study Program : Beginner Level: Pronunciation, Writing, Korean Alphabet, Spelling, Vocabulary, Practice Quiz With Audio Files.

LEARN KOREAN WITH CLASSIC SHORT STORIES

Try learning Korean with classic short stories, with downloadable audio files by a professional Korean voice actor, and side-by-side English-Korean parallel texts!

For complete list of titles, visit **newampersand.com.**

SEOUL KOREA Subway Tour Guide :
How To Enjoy The City's Top 100 Attractions Just By Taking Subway!

ISBN 979-11-88195-84-8

FANDOM MEDIA

For permission requests, write us at

marketing@newampersand.com

www.newampersand.com

Printed in Great Britain
by Amazon

20016370R00059